Suzanne's
Natural Food
Cookbook

Suzanne's Natural Food Cookbook

Suzanne Marquardt
Foreword by David Dodson, M.D.

LANCELOT PRESS
HANTSPORT, NOVA SCOTIA

ISBN 0-88999-328-9
Designed by Robert Pope
Published 1986

Lancelot Press Limited, Hantsport, N.S.
Office and plant situated on Highway No. 1, $1/2$ mile east of Hantsport

This book is dedicated to my mother
whom I love very dearly.

Contents

Acknowledgements

I am very grateful to the following people for their guidance and inspiration — Mrs. Murphy, Robert, Mr. Pope, Daniel, Muriel, Sally, The Macrobiotics East Group, "The Pod," Ek, Werner Erhard, Michio Kushi and Georges Osahwa and to all those who shared their recipes so willingly.

Foreword *by David Dodson, M.D.*

When Suzanne Marquardt asked me to write a foreword to *Suzanne's Natural Food Cookbook*, I was delighted to accept the invitation. These recipes are not only delicious, but those people who adopt her macrobiotic style of cuisine can be assured a major improvement in their health.

Until very recently, mankind's health was primarily threatened by infectious diseases and by nutritional deficiencies. The last few generations have seen remarkable progress in eliminating the old scourges of tuberculosis, smallpox, pellagra, scurvy, dysentry, etc. Unfortunately, we are now plagued with terrible epidemics of coronary artery disease, high blood pressure, cancer, osteoporosis and other chronic ailments.

Many people feel helpless regarding these conditions, thinking for instance that cancer strikes as an act of God against which they are powerless to do anything. Such feelings are perhaps not unreasonable in view of medicine's inability to understand, not to mention control, these serious diseases.

Fortunately, we now know that we are not at all helpless against the modern epidemics of cancer, heart disease, arthritis, diabetes, and other diseases. It is now firmly established that diet plays a major role in causing these so-called degenerative diseases and in protecting us from them — the choice is yours.

The modern diet consumed by wealthy people around the world, but most notably in the developed countries of North America and Northern Europe, have several fatal flaws: far too much fat and far too little whole grains. Our food is also highly processed with the result that we eat too little fresh fruits and vegetables.

Whole grains are excellent sources of vitamins and fiber which are lost when the grains are milled to produce white rice or white flour and baked goods. Although dozens of nutrients are lost in the milling process, when vitamins B_1, B_2, B_3 and iron are added to white flour, it is called "enriched." If this is enriched, then the Pope isn't Catholic, birds don't fly and fish don't swim.

Perhaps the single worst aspect of the modern diet is its high fat content. This is related to the problems of obesity, heart disease, and cancer, among other problems. Why does the modern diet contain 40-50% of its calories from fat? Simply because of excessive consumption of animal foods. For example, though the dairy industry likes to point out that whole milk has only 4% fat, this means 4% by weight. They do not like to point out that milk is mostly water with fat providing about 60% of the calories. Furthermore, dairy foods provide highly saturated fat and cholesterol which are directly responsible for narrowing the arteries, leading to strokes, heart attacks and other serious problems. Meat is also rich in saturated fat and cholesterol, and poultry, though not as bad, again provides about 20% of calories from fat, the fat also being highly saturated.

In contrast, white meat fishes are only about one per cent fat by weight. More importantly, fish fat is different from the fat found in land animals or birds. The fish oils, known as omega 3 fatty acids, actually lower the blood cholesterol and may improve immune function.

Exciting as the knowledge of the latest nutritional data may be, probably the only reason anyone will eat a diet based on whole grains, fresh fruits and vegetables, fish and other natural snacks, drinks and desserts is the reason my family eats this way: the wonderful, wholesome, satisfying taste.

So go ahead, try these recipes. I think you will be amazed at how delicious such natural food tastes. I'm sure the more you adopt the macrobiotic way of eating, the more your health will benefit! Bon apetit!

Dr. Dodson is professor of nutrition at Boston University Medical Centre.

Introduction

One hot August morning I found myself in the kitchen of the Macrobiotic Learning Centre in Boston, Massachusetts. Since that time a major shift has occurred in the way I look at food, and I am very grateful that I was given the opportunity to see nutrition as a basis for health and happiness.

This cookbook is a result of two years of experimenting and exchanging. It is a collection of recipes from a group of people in Halifax, Nova Scotia, who realize how diet affects the quality of our lives. Many of these people belong to the Macrobiotics East Group, a non-profit organization that stands for a great way of life based on macrobiotic principles. The following are some of these principles:

1. Eat local foods in season. Apples, fish, fresh produce such as turnips, squash, kale, carrots and parsnips are available locally in fall and winter; radishes, lettuce, peas, in the spring and summer. Coconuts are great for southern monkeys but not so good for northern reindeer.
2. Choose food that is in its natural state and avoid refined, processed products that have been chemically treated.
3. Eat small quantities. Don't overeat. Excess causes all sorts of distress — such as fat and worry about fat.
4. Chew your food well. Aim for 100 chews per mouthful — you may get in 50. (This takes care of number 3, non?)
5. Do not eat for three hours before retiring and eat only when hungry. (This is not easy in our snack-oriented society).
6. Drink before or after meals, but not during. Drink only when thirsty.
7. Desserts and fruits are best reserved for special occasions.

They can be hard to digest after a good, wholesome meal and are more appreciated by themselves.

8. Eat slowly and with gratitude, reflecting on the origin of the food. This does not mean going off into a cave at supper time but making meal time a special occasion for sharing and being joyous.
9. Reduce your intake of dairy and animal products which are high in fats and, together with flour products, contribute to mucus accumulation in the body.
10. Eat simple foods, arranged attractively with special attention to colour, texture and a variety of tastes.
11. Be reasonable! If you are a disciplined person who can jump in feet first, do it. If you're coming from meat and potato land take it easy. Add something different to your diet every week and soon you will begin to choose rather than eliminate.
12. Get outside — exercise, walk, run, play in the fresh air. Take time for yourself and your own needs.
13. Look at health as a place to come from, not as somewhere to get to some day. You are healthy — you just don't know it.

Macrobiotics is also about balance and harmony. The pie-shaped diagram shown is a general guide as to percentages and proportions. These are daily quantities and each meal should contribute to an overall balance.

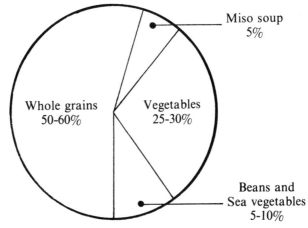

Miso soup
5%

Whole grains
50-60%

Vegetables
25-30%

Beans and
Sea vegetables
5-10%

For more information on macrobiotic philosophy and cooking, please refer to the bibliography at the back of the book, or contact the Macrobiotics East Group, 175 Harlington Crescent, Halifax, Nova Scotia, B3M 3M9; or phone 902-445-4695.

Requests

1. Please read the entire recipe before jumping in to make something. Look up any terms you don't understand in the glossary at the back.
2. Please don't take any ingredient as the absolute gospel be all and end all. Be brave — play with the recipes — experiment, substitute and create. Have fun!
3. Take a minute to give us some feedback. We want to know what worked for you and what didn't, how we botched it, how we didn't. Send all inquiries and requests to Suzanne's Natural Food Cookbook, Lancelot Press, Hantsport, N.S. B0P 1P0

Suzanne Marquardt
Halifax, Nova Scotia
October 19, 1986

Grains

S·K·M

Rice

Basically, there are two kinds of rice — brown and white. White rice is brown rice that has been polished and refined and as such is not really a whole food. We are going to talk about brown rice, of which there are four main types — long grain, medium grain, short grain and sweet brown rice. Long grain is used more often in the summer; medium and short grain are winter varieties. Sweet rice is used mainly for desserts or breakfast because of its sweeter taste or it can be mixed with the other three for variety and a more mellow experience.

Rice is generally found as organic or non-organic. Organic usually means that the rice was cultivated without the addition of man-made chemicals and fertilizers. The best quality of rice is one without a great deal of chipped or broken grains. This condition indicates a poor milling process and exposes the grain to an oxydizing process which can result in loss of minerals and vitamins. Grains are best stored in a cool, dry place in airtight containers. Generally they keep very well for long periods of time; in fact, those discovered in Egyptian tombs are said to have sprouted very easily within a short time of adding water.

Brown rice has a natural balance of minerals, protein and carbohydrates and a high quality protein to make it the most suitable grain for daily consumption. Rice can be combined with legumes and dairy products to increase its protein utilization. The addition of other whole grains — wheat berries, whole oats and rye or corn — makes for an interesting variation. Lightly roasting any grain in a dry skillet before cooking will add a rich, nutty flavour and texture.

Basic Brown Rice — Pressure Cooking Method

2 cups Brown rice
3-4 cups water
pinch of sea salt per cup of rice

If the rice is very dirty you may wish to place it on a plate before washing and pick out any stones or uninvited guests. Wash the grain by gently stirring with your hand in a counter-clockwise direction (if you want to be a purist) and then drain off the water. Repeat three or more times until the water becomes almost clear. Place in a strainer and rinse quickly to remove any remaining dust. Place rice in pressure cooker. Add 1 1/2 to 2 cups of water per cup of rice depending on your cooker, your stove and the humidity. You will probably have to experiment a few times before you arrive at just the right formula. Bring the rice slowly to a boil using a medium to high heat and then add a small pinch of salt for every cup of rice used. Place the cover on the cooker and turn the flame to high (bring to pressure). When the gauge begins to hiss or jiggle, transfer the pot to another burner with a flame deflector on top of the burner and reduce heat to medium-low (just high enough to keep the gauge gently hissing). Electric stoves usually do not require the use of flame tamers; simply lower the heat under the pot. Cook for 40-45 minutes. When done, remove from heat and bring pressure down. Placing a chopstick under the gauge will produce a lighter, fluffier rice. Letting the pressure come down gradually by itself without a chopstick gives the rice a more peaceful feeling.

Boiled Brown Rice

1 cup brown rice
2 cups water or vegetable stock
pinch sea salt

Wash rice as for pressure-cooking recipe. Bring water or stock to boil in a saucepan with a tight-fitting lid. Pour grain in slowly, stirring as you go, and add a pinch of salt per cup of grain. Turn heat down so as to maintain a gentle simmer. Cover and cook on lowest temperature until all the water is absorbed (45 minutes to 1 hour). If not quite done, add a little boiling water and continue cooking. Do not stir any more than necessary as this can produce gummy rice. Let rice sit approximately ten minutes covered before serving.

Don't stop at plain brown rice. Let your imagination run wild! Sauté raw grain dry or in oil with chopped onion, celery or green pepper before adding boiling water; try different herbs and spices; stir-fry with vegetables, garnish with roasted pumpkin seeds, sunflower or sesame seeds with a touch of tamari sauce, sprinkle with nuts, serve with sauces or gravies, use leftovers in casseroles or combine with your favourite bean burger recipe.

Fried Rice (serves 2)

2 cups cooked rice
1/2 medium onion
2 carrots
4-5 kale leaves or mustard greens or any green vegetable
sesame oil
1/2 tsp. tahini

Slice onions in crescent moon shapes and the carrots thinly on the diagonal or in matchsticks. Chop the greens in one inch pieces. Lightly brush a cast iron or stainless steel skillet with the oil. Sauté the onions in the oil until transluscent; add carrots and sauté until soft. Put in rice and a dash of tamari and 2-3 tbsps. of stock, water or leftover soup broth. Simmer gently for 5-10 minutes. Add kale and continue cooking another 3-4 minutes, covered, until kale is a brilliant green. Don't leave too long, as kale will turn a sickly green colour. Parsnips, cauliflower, peppers or any vegetable can be substituted for the carrots and kale, keeping in mind colours and texture. Barley and millet can be prepared in the same way. Herbs and spices can be added according to taste and preferences.

Millet

Millet forms a major part of the diet of about one-third of the world's population. It is widely used in China, Japan, Korea, India and Africa. It provides well-balanced, low-gluten protein, calcium, iron and lecithin. It can be used in place of rice in almost any recipe although it tends to be drier and not as flavourful by itself.

Millet is easily recognizable by its tiny, circular yellow grains. Roasting the grains before boiling adds a rich, nutty taste.

Cooked Millet

1 cup millet
2 cups water

Wash millet by placing in a large bowl and swirling water around gently several times until water is relatively clear. Place in a strainer and quickly rinse off any remaining dust. Put millet in a pre-heated cast iron dutch oven, frying pan or heavy sauce pan and roast gently until a fragrant, nutty aroma arises and/or the grains turn a golden brown colour and begin to pop. Gradually add 2 cups of boiling water and a pinch of salt per cup of millet, stirring if necessary. Cover and cook undisturbed for 30 minutes. Remove from heat and let sit 10-15 minutes before serving. Millet is a dry, fluffy grain that takes to sauces and gravies very nicely. A simple but tasty sauce can be made by sautéing a handful of sliced onion in sesame oil until soft and adding a tsp. of tamari, 1 tsp. tahini plus 1/4 cup vegetable stock or leftover soup. Add cooked millet and stir until most of sauce is absorbed.

Millet With Sweet Vegetables

1 cup millet
1 medium carrot, sliced 1/4" thick
1 medium onion, crescent moon slices
pinch sea salt
2 cups boiling water

Wash millet. Lightly brush sesame oil in the bottom of a pot. Sauté onions for about 3 minutes, add carrots and sauté for another 5 minutes. Add millet and sauté for 3 minutes, stirring to avoid burning. Add the boiling water and sea salt. Bring to a boil, cover, reduce heat to low and simmer 30-35 minutes until all the water is absorbed. Leave covered 10 minutes before serving. Cauliflower, squash or any sweet vegetable lends itself well to millet and may be substituted for carrot.

Millet and Squash

This is an absolutely superb dish which we first heard of from Lois Thompson of Woodstock, New Brunswick. It is incredibly sweet and satisfying as a main course or a dessert.

1/2 cup millet
a pinch of salt
1 small winter squash
1 1/2 cups water
handful almonds or pecans, roasted

Wash millet and dry roast in a cast iron frying pan. Place in pressure cooker with 1 1/2 cups water. Cut up washed squash with skin into bite-size pieces. Add to millet with a pinch of salt. Bring to pressure and cook for 20 minutes. Without a pressure cooker this recipe will take twice the cooking time or until squash and millet are soft. Allow pressure to come down and mash millet and squash with a potato masher. Place in a loaf pan or cake pan to set. When cool and jelled, decorate with roasted nuts and cut into squares. Serve at room temperature.

Millet and Cauliflower — mashed potatoes

1 cup millet
1 cup cauliflower flowerettes and pieces
1/2 onion, diced or sliced
3 cups boiling water
2 tsps. sesame oil

Wash millet. Lightly brush sesame oil in the bottom of a pot. Sauté onions for about 3 minutes, add cauliflower and millet and sauté for another 3 minutes, stirring to avoid scorching. Add boiling water and salt, cover and reduce heat to low. Simmer for 30-35 minutes until millet is cooked. The mixture will be fairly liquid. Mash everything together to obtain a potato-like consistency and serve as you would mashed potatoes.

Barley

Barley is believed to be one of the oldest of the cultivated grains. It is a relative of the rice plant and is grown as a staple in the Far East, Asia, Middle East, Europe and South America. It is the most important food in Tibet, and is also grown in North America, where it is used mostly in making beer and alcohol and for feeding livestock. By itself, barley is quite bland but it combines well with other grains and is especially good with beans and vegetables in soups and stews. Barley has a cooling effect on the body and is thus a good summer grain. It is a good source of iron, calcium, potassium and phosphorus, as well as vitamins B_1 and B_2. The sprouted kernels form the malt which we know as barley malt and roasted sprouts are ground and used as a coffee substitute.

Barley soup is gentle and revitalizing to the stomach and digestive system. Barley flour is very good in breads and pastries. The kernels make a delicious tea when roasted with the hulls on and boiled in water. The Japanese people drink barley tea, called mugicha.

Whole grain, hulled barley is the best source of nutrients. Pearling removes the outer portions of the kernel and the hull. What remains after the first 3 pearlings is sold as Scotch or pot barley; pearl barley is what remains after six pearlings, having lost about 74% of the protein, 85% of the fat, 97% of the fibre and 88% of the original minerals.[1]

1.   Harris and von Loesecke, *Nutritional Evaluation of Food Processing.*

Pressure Cooked Brown Rice and Barley (serves 4-6)

2 and 1/3 cups organic brown rice
2/3 cup whole, organic barley
3 3/4 to 4 1/2 cups water or vegetable stock (1 1/4 to 1 1/2 cups of water per cup of grain)

Wash rice and barley and place in a pressure cooker. Add water and bring to a boil. Add 3 pinches of salt, cover and bring to pressure. Cook for 40 minutes on low heat. Bring pressure down. Remove grain and serve.

The barley and rice may also be boiled using 2 cups of water to 1 cup of grain. The barley can be soaked for 4-6 hours before cooking. Measure the soaking water and count this as part of the total cooking water.

Robert's Barley Loaf (serves 4)

2 tbsp. chopped parsley
1 carrot, diced
1 onion, diced
1/2 tsp. sesame oil
1 tbsp. tamari
1 cup barley
1/2 cup green lentils
5 cups water or vegetable stock
1/4 cup roasted almonds.

Sauté onion and carrot in the sesame oil. Add 1 tbsp. tamari and the chopped parsley. Wash barley and lentils separately and mix in with the vegetables. Add water and bring to a boil. Reduce heat and simmer 2 minutes. Pour the mixture into an oiled casserole dish or loaf pan. Preheat oven to 350⁰. Bake covered for one hour. Roast almonds, slice and decorate loaf before serving.

Buckwheat

Buckwheat is still a staple grain in parts of Europe, Poland and Russia, where it is eaten in its whole form and in Japan, where it has been used to make noodles called *soba*. Many Jewish people use buckwheat in making knishes or in kasha varnitchkes. It is also a principal ingredient in cabbage rolls. Any Hungarian, Jewish or Russian cookbook will have numerous recipes that you can adapt to your own likes and dislikes.

Buckwheat is eaten mainly during the fall and winter as it tends to generate body heat and is known for its strengthening qualities.

It is available in a roasted and unroasted form. The roasted variety should be re-roasted for only 3-5 minutes before use; the unroasted kind should be roasted in a dry skillet for 10-15 minutes, stirring to avoid burning. Ask for the cracked buckwheat known as kasha.

Buckwheat and kasha are very high in protein, calcium, iron, vitamin B and other minerals. Like millet, they tend to be fairly dry when cooked and need a simple sauce and vegetables to tone down a somewhat earthy, strong taste. The sauce recipes which follow can be used with most grains, vegetables and casseroles.

Cracked Buckwheat or Kasha

1 cup groats
2 cups water or vegetable stock
a pinch of salt

Boil water. In a separate pan, toast groats. Add the boiling water to the groats and a pinch of salt. Cover with a lid and simmer for 20 minutes or until all the liquid has been absorbed. Serve with vegetables and tamari or use one of the sauces included in this chapter. A simple sauce made from blending 1 tbsp. miso, 3 tsp. lemon juice, 1 tsp. of tahini and enough cold water to make a creamy consistency is good with kasha. Try a touch of thyme for a unique taste.

Kasha Croquettes

3 cups cooked kasha
1/3 cup onions, chopped
1 bunch scallions, chopped
1 medium carrot, diced
pinch salt
whole wheat flour for binding

Mix ingredients, finishing with the flour. Make 2 inch balls. Flatten to one inch and fry in 1/4 inch of oil. Serve hot with a few drops of soya or tamari sauce or use with the zucchini-onion mixture in the following recipe.

Baked Croquettes

3 cups cooked kasha
1/3 cup onions, chopped
1/4 green pepper, diced and sautéed
1/2 cup matzoh meal or oat flakes
pinch salt
3 large zucchini, sliced
2 tbsp. oil, olive is good
2 onions, chopped
1 cup stock or water
2-3 tsp. tamari

To make the balls, blend kasha, onions, green pepper, oatmeal and salt. Form small balls. Place on an oiled baking sheet and bake at 375⁰ for 1/2 hour. In the meantime, sauté onions, then zucchini in the olive oil. After 5 minutes, add water and tamari; simmer for 5 minutes covered. Add baked balls; place them over the vegetable mixture and allow to cook covered for 10-15 minutes over a low flame.

Sauce Bechamel

2 tbsp. sweet rice flour (or whole wheat or white)
1 tbsp. sesame butter or tahini
1/2 onion, chopped
1-2 scallion tops, chopped or chives

pinch salt or few drops of tamari
1 1/2-2 cups water or vegetable sauce — boiling
1 tsp. oil

In a heavy saucepan or skillet, sauté onion and scallions in oil. Add flour, sesame butter and salt (if tahini or sesame butter is too thick, dilute in 2 tbsp. of boiling water before adding.) Pour the rest of the water in very slowly, stirring constantly to maintain an even thick mixture. When creamy and smooth, simmer for 10-15 minutes over a low flame, half-covered with a lid. Variations: Use unbleached white flour or toasted whole wheat or oat flour. Lightly toasted barley flour is good as well. A pinch of nutmeg, coriander, basil, thyme or dill produces a totally different taste. A cup of mashed chickpeas, lentils or aduki beans provides interesting flavour and texture. Add these to the basic finished sauce with extra stock or water if necessary.

Mushroom Sauce

1/2 lb. mushrooms, sliced
1 tsp. sesame oil
1 clove garlic, crushed (optional)
3 cups water, stock or leftover soup broth
2-3 tsps barley miso
2 heaping tablespoons kuzu or arrowroot
1-2 tbsp. tahini
1 tsp. lemon juice
1 tsp. finely chopped fresh basil (optional)

Sauté mushrooms in oil. Add the garlic and then the water or other liquid. Let simmer for a few minutes or until mushrooms are tender. Dilute miso in a little broth and add to mushrooms. Dilute kuzu or arrowroot in a little cold water and stir into sauce. Simmer just until thick and clear. Stir in tahini and simmer a few more minutes. Add basil or herbs. This sauce can be prepared in advance and heated up just before serving. Add a little lemon juice for extra flavour.

Miso Gravy

1 1/2 tbsp. olive or sesame oil
1 onion, diced
1-2 cloves garlic, minced
3 tbsp. whole wheat or unbleached flour
3 tbsp. Brewer's yeast (optional)
1 and 2/3 cups water stock (approx.)
2-3 tsp. barley miso
1/4 tsp. dried basil
fresh parsley (optional)
1 tbsp. white wine or mirin (optional)

Heat oil in a medium-sized skillet. Add onion and garlic and sauté over medium heat for three to five minutes. Lower heat and add flour and yeast. Stir constantly for about one minute, then slowly add 1 1/2 cups stock while stirring briskly. Stir until mixture begins to thicken. Combine miso with 2-3 tbsp. of hot water; add along with the basil and parsley and mirin. Simmer, uncovered, for about 15 minutes, stirring occasionally. Serve hot. If gravy is too thin, slowly add 1 tbsp. arrowroot or kuzu dissolved in 1 or 2 tbsp. cold water.

NOTE: Generally all sauces are high in calories and oil and therefore should be used sparingly and for special occasions. Tamari, stock and arrowroot or kuzu can be just as tasty and are better for more frequent use. Vegetables such as squash and carrots can be puréed and used as sauces as well as split peas, red lentils, adukis and chick peas, which can double as sauces when diluted with their own cooking stock and sprinkled with herbs, onions or garlic. Experiment!

Stuffed Cabbage Rolls (6-8 servings)

1 medium head cabbage (Chinese cabbage rolls very well)
2 cups cooked rice and 1 cup cooked buckwheat (kasha)
1 cup cooked aduki beans or lentils
3 tbsp. whole wheat pastry flour
1/2 cup onions, chopped
1/2 cup carrots, diced or grated
2 tbsp. oil
salt to taste
1/2 cup pine nuts (optional)
3 tsp. tamari and 1 tbsp. tahini diluted in 1/3 cup stock or water
2 cups bechamel sauce (p. 25)

Remove core from cabbage (if not using Chinese variety). Steam whole cabbage for 10-15 minutes over boiling water, or until leaves peel off easily. Carefully remove 15-20 outer leaves. Let cool slightly. Sauté onions and carrots. Combine rice, kasha, beans, flour and sautéd vegetables. Season to taste with salt or your favourite herbs. Thyme and rosemary are good. Place 2 tbsp. of this mixture on top of each cabbage leaf. Fold in sides neatly; roll cabbage and close like an envelope. Fasten with a toothpick if necessary. Place in a casserole pan. Pour tahini-tamari sauce over them. Bake covered at 375⁰ for 30-40 minutes (depending on type and thickness of cabbage). Remove, cover with bechamel sauce and broil for 2-3 minutes or until top is slightly scorched.

Sauce variations include your favourite tomato sauce or vegetable stock flavoured with a bit of miso or tamari and onions. In this case, spread half the sauce in the bottom of a lightly greased baking dish; place stuffed leaves seam-side down over sauce and add the rest of sauce. Cover and bake for 45 minutes or simmer gently on top of the stove for 45 minutes. Here the oven is at 350⁰.

Cabbage rolls are a good family project. They taste much better the second day, so if you can possibly prepare them in advance without devouring them the same day, the wait is worth it.

Bulgur and Vegetables

1 cup bulgur, washed
2 cups boiling water, stock or soup
diced parsnip and carrot
diced small onion
tamari to taste
tahini, 1 tsp. (optional)

Dry roast the bulgur or lightly sauté grain and vegetables in 1
tsp. sesame oil (not the greens). Add 2 cups boiling water.
Simmer gently 15-20 minutes until liquid is absorbed.
Vegetable stock or leftover miso soup gives an excellent
flavour. Add tamari to taste and tahini if desired. Top with
parsley and greens and serve hot or warm. This makes an
excellent light summer dish.

Rosemary's Time (serves 4)

1 cup raw bulgur
2 cups boiling water
3-4 chopped scallions
2 medium carrots
4-8 oz. tofu
1 tsp. sesame oil
2 pinches rosemary
parsley and/or watercress

Dry roast bulgur. Add 2 cups boiling stock or water and cook
until liquid is absorbed (15-20 minutes). Slice carrots into
matchsticks or small thin pieces. Chop scallions, parsley and
watercress into small pieces. Sauté carrots in 1 tsp. sesame oil.
Stir in scallions, bulgur and rosemary. Place tofu on top.
Steam 10-15 minutes or until tofu is cooked. Add tamari near
the end of cooking. Garnish with parsley and watercress.

Cooking Whole Grains, Flakes, and Cereals

Grain (1 cup dry)	Regular Cooking		Pressure Cooking	
	water (cups)	time (min.)	water (cups)	time (min.)
Barley	2 1/2	60	2	40
Porridge	4-5	90	NO*	
Buckwheat Groats, Kasha	2-2 1/2	20-25	NO	
Corn meal, yellow	4	30	NO	
Millet, whole	3 1/2	30	3	25
Porridge	5	60	NO	
Oats, whole or groats	3	60	2 1/2	45
Porridge	5	2 1/2 hours	NO	
Flaked, Rolled,	3	30	NO	
Oatmeal	3	30	NO	
Rice				
Short grain	2 1/2	50	2	40-60
Medium grain	2	50	1 1/2	40-60
Long grain	1 1/2	40-50	1 1/4	30-40
Porridge	5	90	NO	
Rice cream	4	30	NO	
Flaked	2	20	NO	
Rye, whole or groats	2 1/2	60	2	45
Flaked	2	20	NO	
Wheat Berries	2 1/2	60	2	45
Porridge	5 1/2	2 1/2 hours	NO	
Cracked wheat	3	20-25	NO	
Bulgur	2	15-20	NO	
Flaked	2	20	NO	

Seasoning: pinch sea salt per cup of dry grain.

Yield: 1 cup of dry whole grain makes approximately 2 1/2 cups of cooked grain.

* Do *not* pressure cook cereals or porridge; they may clog up the vent on top of the pressure cooker.

Equivalent Table uncooked to cooked

Grain
(1 cup dry)

Yield

Grain (1 cup dry)	Yield
Barley (whole)	3 1/2 c.
Buckwheat (kasha)	2 1/2 c
Bulgur Wheat	2 1/2 c.
Cracked Wheat	2 1/3 c.
Millet	3 1/2 c.
Coarse cornmeal (polenta)	3 c.
Brown Rice	3 c.
Wild Rice	4 c.
Whole wheat berries	2 2/3 c.
Black Beans	2 c.
Black-eyed peas	2 c.
Garbanzos (chick peas)	2 c.
Kidney beans	2 c.
Lentils & split peas	2 1/4 c.
Limas	1 1/4 c.
Baby limas	1 3/4 c.
Pinto beans	2 c.
Red beans	2 c.
Small white beans (navy, etc.)	2 c.
Soy beans	2 c.
Soy grits	2 c.

Vegetables

Vegetables

Vegetables are a greatly neglected but very important part of our diet. About 25-30% of a vegetarian diet should consist of vegetables. (see circle on page 12). Fresh produce is preferable to canned or frozen for reasons of nutrition and vitality. The following is a list of nutritious, fortifying vegetables. We have excluded those of a tropical origin as it is more strengthening to eat food that is locally grown and cultivated in a region of similar climatic conditions.

Green Leafy Vegetables

Arugula
Bok Choy
Carrot Tops
Celery leaves
Chinese Cabbage
Collard Greens
Dandelion Greens
Endive
Escarole
Kale
Lambsquarters

Leeks
Lettuce
Mustard Greens
Parsley
Radish Tops
Scallion
Sprouts
Swiss Chard
Turnip Greens
Watercress

Stem/Root Vegetables

Burdock
Carrots
Daikon
Dandelion Root
Lotus Root
Onion

Radish
Rutabaga
Salsify
Turnip
Parsnip

Ground Vegetables

Cauliflower	Mushrooms
Broccoli	Pumpkin
Celery	Squash — winter and summer
Brussel Sprouts	Wax or yellow beans
Cabbage — green and red	Zucchini — green and yellow
Green Peas	

Leafy Greens

The appearance of greens suggests many of the qualities they impart to the person consuming them. The colour green is one of peace and serenity. The leafy expansive nature is indicative of a lightness and upward, rising energy.

Most greens take just a few minutes to cook and are prepared just before sitting down to a meal. Rinse them carefully in cool water to eliminate all sand and grit. Tear them by hand if possible or cook the leaves whole and slice after cooking. Avoid adding salt while cooking except for kale and collard, as it can produce a bitter taste. Lemon juice or rice vinegar goes especially well with kale and collard greens.

How to Cook Greens

1. Boil 1/4 to 1/2 inch of water. Dip in greens and boil on high heat until just tender and still bright green. Chopsticks are a good utensil to use here. 2. Place washed greens in a steamer and steam for 2-5 minutes. 3. Sauté in 1-2 tbsp. of water or 1 tsp. sesame oil. Cover and simmer on low heat until brightly coloured and tender.

Steamed Kale

Kale is a wonderful representative of the green family. One cup cooked provides 5 grams of protein, 1.4 grams of fibre (the same as 1/2 cup bran flakes and 100 times the amount found in a slice of whole wheat bread), 9130 I.U. of Vitamin A., 102 mg Vitamin C, 206 mg calcium and 1.8 mg iron.

Of particular note is the protein and calcium content. Very few vegetables contain any protein at all and greens rate second only to sea vegetables for high plant-quality calcium. Kale is a very hardy plant and will grow even under winter snow conditions. In fact, winter and spring kale are usually the most tender and the sweetest.

Wash kale well. Cut off stems and boil them separately with a pinch of sea salt for about 3-5 minutes. Dip leaves in boiling water for 1-3 minutes or place on top of stems after 3 minutes and boil for the last 2-3 minutes with the stems.

Yellow and Greens

Add greens to vegetables such as carrots or squash during the last five minutes of cooking.

Green is for Garnish

Any leafy green vegetable can be finely chopped and used to enhance the colour and presentation of soups, salads, rice or vegetable dishes. Carrot tops are especially nice when added to cooked carrots or soup. Cooking the edible tops of any plant with a root provides a good balance and harmony between the two extremes of the plant.

Root Vegetables

Root vegetables are very compact and strengthening. We tend to eat more of them in the winter time when we need more heat and a counteracting force to the expansive nature of the cold temperature outside the body. Also, root vegetables keep well during the winter months and we can eat local varieties until spring. The most popular group includes daikon radish, parsnips, carrots, turnips, rutabaga and beets. Potatoes, tomatoes and eggplants are tropical in origin. They do grow in our climate but are more at home in much warmer climates. Overconsumption can be weakening to the system.

Squash

Squash is such a unique vegetable that it deserves a special category of its own. Store this vegetable at room temperature in a dry place and you will have local produce all year round. The skin can be eaten, especially on young, first crops. If not organic or waxed, discard the skin after baking. Most squash is very sweet and can satisfy a craving for desserts. Squash or pumpkin pies can be made with very little sweetener and the seeds dried and roasted for snacks.

How to Preserve Fresh Vegetable Nutrients

Scrub with a natural bristle brush under running cold water for root vegetables. For leafy ones, rinse quickly and pat dry. Wait until just before eating or cooking to wash. Store in plastic bags in the crisper of refrigerator. A cold, slightly humid environment is best for highly perishable foods. Leafy greens store well in closed brown paper bags. Store fruits and vegetables apart from one another. Gases and strong flavours can affect tastes. If vegetables such as carrots, parsnips, etc. are not organic you may wish to peel them. Avoid peeling or trimming until just before cooking as valuable minerals and vitamins will oxydize or if possible peel after cooking to prevent leaching of nutrients into the water. Use trimmings to make stocks and save any water left over from steaming or sautéing to make sauces and to boil grains. Avoid exposing vegetables to air and light for long periods of time. The more pieces you cut a vegetable into and the longer you leave out uncovered, the more nutrients are lost. If the vegetable is to be cooked but served cold, cut or slice it after you cook it. Buy vegetables that are exactly the size you need for one meal and use the whole food. Avoid buying plastic wrapped halves which will have lost considerable nutrients already.

Cooking Vegetables

The best way to cook just-picked vegetables is the simplest. Any pot will continue to cook a vegetable after the heat's been turned off so take it off before you think it's done.

Steaming

Use a collapsible steamer basket, bamboo steamer or metal sieve and a saucepan with a tight-fitting lid. Bring an inch or two of water to a boil, put in the basket and place vegetables in the basket, replacing the lid. Drop the heat just enough to keep the water bubbling. Vegetables cook very quickly this way, probably no longer than ten minutes. You will know they are cooked when a fork or point of a knife enters without much difficulty. Avoid overcooking vegetables as they are not only unattractive but can create acidity when not chewed well. Stainless steel or cast-iron enamelled pots are best. Most vegetables can be steamed with no problem.

Waterless Method

Here a pan which distributes heat evenly all around and has a close-fitting lid is best. Preheat the pot and place two tablespoons of water in it to provide steam until the vegetables release their own. When the water boils, add vegetables, cover and turn the heat down low after a couple of minutes. Cooking time will be longer than with steaming. Instead of water, you may sauté lightly in a small amount of oil and add a very small amount of water (about 2 tbsp.) after sautéing and proceed as above. Vegetables done this way may be stirred occasionally or shake the pan in a counter-clockwise circle now and then. Add salt or soya just before done — 5 minutes before the end. Depending on the size of the pieces, it should take 30-45 minutes on a very low heat. This method approximates the French method 'à l'etuvée' whereby the vegetables "sweat" so that they cook themselves in the water vapour they're giving up. It applies well to carrots, turnips, green peas and snap beans.

Sautéing

Cut vegetables into matchsticks, thin slices or shave them (like sharpening a pencil). Brush a skillet with a small amount of sesame oil or safflower oil. Heat the oil. Add the vegetables and a pinch of salt to bring out their natural sweetness. Sauté by occasionally moving from side to side with chopsticks or a wooden spoon. Sauté for 5 minutes on a medium flame. Reduce to low and sauté for another 10 minutes gently mixing to avoid burning. Season with sea salt or tamari and sauté 2-3 minutes longer and serve.

For the same size vegetables or even larger, thicker pieces, first sauté in a small amount of oil over a medium flame for about five minutes. Then add 2-3 tablespoons of stock or water and cook until tender.

Possible Variations for Sautéing

Onions-carrots-cabbage. Cook onions first until they change colour and then add other vegetables. Scallions-carrots-watercress — scallions first, carrots (diced) and watercress very briefly. Scallions-carrots-boiled chick-peas — very good with cooked rice. Scallions first, then carrots, then chick-peas. Avoid chick-peas that are too soft. Scallions-zucchini-celery; Onions-string beans-carrots; Onions-brussel sprouts-carrots; Onions-cauliflower-carrots; Parsley-carrots; Onions-parsnips-carrots or parsnips-carrots-burdock; Swiss chard and tofu; Kale and carrots; Chinese cabbage, mushrooms and tofu.

Baking

Baking vegetables is usually done in the fall or winter when it is colder outside and a hot oven warms up the kitchen but also because the quality of the vegetable is more warming. The most commonly baked vegetables are squash and root varieties.

Baked Carrots

4 large carrots
sesame or safflower oil
casserole with a lid — pyrex, cast iron, clay baker

Slither carrots lengthwise in quarters or eighths. You may lightly oil either the vegetables or the casserole. Place boiling water to just cover the bottom of the dish. Bake at 325⁰ for one hour to 1 1/4 hours, checking periodically for "doneness" and water level. Don't drown them as some water will evaporate from the carrots themselves and add to the cooking liquid. Barley or rice malt may be added halfway through for a sweet treat.

Baked Squash

Everyone loves baked squash! We find the turban-topped buttercup to be the sweetest in our region, but other varieties are equally tasty in season. Depending on your appetite, one medium squash usually will feed four people.

Cut the vegetable into two pieces, oil the outside and the cookie sheet on which it is to be baked. Place hollow side down in a 375⁰-400⁰ oven for 45-60 minutes. Cooking time varies with size. Rub a pinch of salt on the inside or add tamari when 3/4 cooked *or* forget the salt and serve with umeboshi plum paste. When just about done, turn over the squash and allow it to turn slightly brown.

Stuffed Baked Squash

one medium-large squash
1 cup cooked millet, rice, wild rice or any grain
1 small onion, diced
4-5 fresh mushrooms, diced
1/2 stalk celery, diced
1/4 cup carrot, chopped fine
water
tamari or sea salt

Cut squash in two and remove seeds. Oil the outside and the

baking dish. Combine millet (grain) and diced vegetables. You may wish to lightly sauté the vegetables beforehand in a small amount of sesame oil. Add a few drops of water to moisten. Fill up each hollow of the squash and place in a baking dish with a cover. Bake at 375^0-400^0 for 35-40 minutes. Bake another ten minutes uncovered.

Carrot Pie

2 cups flour
1/4 cup corn oil
water to make it stick together
pinch of salt

Filling

3 bunches carrots — approximately 2 lbs. cut into 1 inch chunks
2 medium onions cut into slices
1 tbsp. sesame oil

Sauté onions and carrots in oil. Add water or stock to cook. Cover the vegetables half way up with stock and cook until tender. Add salt or tamari to taste plus 1 tsp. cinnamon or less. Purée in blender until smooth and pour into pie crust. Bake at 400^0 for 10 minutes and 375^0 for 30 minutes. Oat flakes and/or sesame seeds can be sprinkled on top before baking or you may wish to add a lattice crust. Squash or parsnips can be substituted for the carrots.

No Tomato Sauce

This sauce is delicious over noodles, polenta or croquettes.

1 or 2 beets, cut into thin slices (if you like beets, use 2)
2 zucchini, cut into slices
2 onions, chopped
2 tablespoons brown rice flour or kuzu
1/2 tsp. salt
1 tbsp. olive or corn oil
1 tbsp. soya sauce or tamari
pinch garlic and oregano

3 cups water or mild stock
1 tbsp. parsley, chopped

In a heavy saucepan, sauté scallions and onions in oil for two minutes; add zucchini, sauté 2 minutes more, then add beets. Simmer five minutes while stirring with a wooden spoon. Add one cup of water or stock and bring to a boil. Simmer 20 minutes covered. Allow to cool for a while and then purée in an electric blender or suribachi. Pour into saucepan. Dilute rice flour in two cups water. Pour mixture into saucepan, add tamari or salt. Bring to a quick boil and simmer ten minutes. Add garlic, oregano and parsley. Cook ten more minutes. For variation, use 1 butternut squash instead of beets for a sweet and golden sauce.

Onions Vichy

This recipe was inspired by some left over mineral water. It turned out to be one of our favourites.

1-2 small onions per person
1-2 cups mineral water or stock
tamari to taste

Peel the onions and make a cross in the root end. Place upright (cross end down) in a dutch oven. Cover the bottom of the pan with mineral water. Simmer until onions are soft and sweet — approximately 30-40 minutes. Add a drop of tamari near the end of cooking.

Onion Pie makes two large pies

6 cups chopped onions
1 tbsp. sesame oil
1 tbsp. umeboshi paste or natto miso
1-2 tbsp. tahini
2 tbsp. kuzu or arrowroot flour
2 tbsp. water

Pastry Pie Crust

3 cups whole wheat pastry flour
1/2 tsp. salt
1/2 cup cold corn oil
1/3 cup cold water

Combine the flour and salt. With a fork, slowly mix in the oil and the water. The dough should be a bit crumbly. Gather into a firm ball. Leave in the bowl and cover with a damp towel. Refrigerate twenty minutes. Divide into two balls. Roll out one of the pieces to a 10-11 inch diameter. Place in a pyrex pie plate. Prick bottom and sides with a fork. Roll out the second ball of dough and use as a lattice covering.
Sauté onions in oil for a few minutes. Add salt, cover and cook 45 minutes, adding a touch of water if necessary. Dilute tahini with ume paste and water to make a pourable sauce or use natto miso or regular rice or soybean miso and dilute tahini with that and some water. Add the onions. Mix kuzu with 2-4 tbsp. of cold water. Cook until thick and clear (5 minutes). Cool slightly. Add to onions. Fill your favourite pie crust (or use above recipe). Do not pre-bake pie crust. Criss cross with strips of dough for an attractive vegetable pie effect. Bake at 350⁰ until done (30-60 minutes). Steamed squash slices are a nice addition. Just layer on top of onions before adding lattice and baking.

Miso Turnips (4-6 servings)

Nikola surprised us all at a potluck with this ingenious method of cooking turnips.

3 small turnips
miso (we used barley)

Peel the turnips. Drill a small hole not quite all the way through with a potato peeler or knife. Fill the hole with your favourite miso and place in a large pot so that the turnips are free standing. Put in enough water to come about half way up the turnips. Place a tight-fitting lid on the pot and steam until tender. This will take about 20-30 minutes or longer, depending on the size of the turnips. Larger turnips may be used and cut into smaller block-like pieces.

Parsnip Chips

These are sweet and crispy and a favourite snack. They take a bit of work — oh those matchsticks — but are well worth the effort.

as many parsnips as you would like to tackle
sesame oil

Scrub parsips well or peel if waxed. Cut into diagonal pieces and then into thin matchsticks. The finished product should resemble shoestring potato chips. Oil a baking sheet and spread out parsnips on the sheet. Bake at 350^0 until crisp and brown.

Parsnips à la mode

Scrub parsnips. Slice lengthwise if thick and cook or steam until tender. Remove from pan and place in a flat casserole dish. Sprinkle with salt (very lightly). Add honey, rice syrup or maple syrup and cinnamon (optional) and bake at 350^0 for 10-15 minutes or until browned. Serve hot or cool.

Summer Salads

Summer can be very hot and humid and we naturally turn towards a lighter, more airy type of vegetable to balance the weather surrounding us. Salads and aspics are a cooling alternative and shorten time spent indoors in the kitchen. What a great opportunity to savour the full flavour of vegetables fresh from the garden.

Vegetable Aspic

An aspic is a jellied, vegetable salad. Aspics are a work of art and great care should be exercised in arranging and choosing colours and textures. Don't overcrowd them, a few varieties are enough. Broccoli and carrots go nicely together as do corn and carrots, corn and broccoli, green and yellow beans.

3 cups vegetables
water or vegetable stock

agar agar flakes

Wash vegetables and cut into thin slices. Cook until just tender and place in a mold or deep dish. Using the cooking water plus enough additional water to cover the vegetables, add 1 tablespoon of agar flakes for each cup of liquid and bring to a boil; simmer until agar is dissolved. Pour over the vegetables and cool in fridge until solidified. One teaspoon of grated ginger or horseradish plus 1 to 1 1/2 tablespoons tamari may be added to the stock for variation. Keep stalks on the broccoli and pack vegetables well to keep them from floating away. A variation on the above method is to cool the agar mixture 15-20 minutes in the refrigerator or until the kanten begins to thicken and then fold in vegetables and transfer to a mold or bowl. Unmold when thoroughly jelled.

Super Salad (serves 4)

2-3 leaves of Chinese cabbage or bok choy
4-5 leaves green lettuce of your choice
1-2 chopped scallions
3 small carrots, thin diagonals or matchsticks
1 small zucchini, sliced
1 small tomato, chunks or slices
1/2 cup left over grain — rice and barley, bulgur, etc. or cold pasta
4-5 roasted walnuts, chopped
handful roasted sunflower and pumpkin seeds

Toss and serve with lemon juice or horseradish dressing.

Horseradish Mustard Dressing

3 tbsp. olive oil
1 tbsp. lemon juice or rice vinegar (or more to taste)
1-2 tsp. horseradish mustard or Dijon mustard mixed with powdered wasabi, a Japanese horseradish

Mix all ingredients well. Pour over salad, grain and vegetables or seaweed dishes.

Pressed Salad

See Pressed Pickles, p. 86

Cucumber Wakame Salad

see Pickle Section

Soups

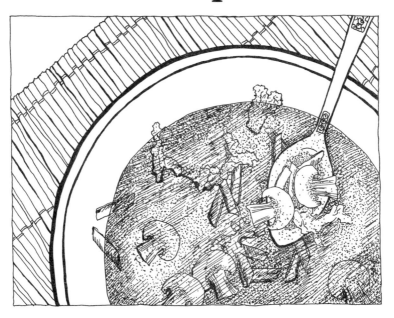

Miso Soup

Miso soup is a mystical experience. Even non-vegetarians agree on this point. Japanese mythology suggests that miso was a gift from the Gods to provide long life and good health. The next time you are feeling off centre or irritable, make up a simple miso soup with a few of your favourite vegetables and take stock of the changes that begin to occur in your sense of well-being. It is most remarkable, like a deep-breathing exercise.

Miso is a puréed, paste-like substance made from fermented, aged soybeans, grain, salt, water and a starter called koji. Its texture is somewhat like a smooth peanut butter and it comes in various colours and consistencies. The most commonly used misos in North America are barley miso which ranges from a reddish brown to a dark brown colour, rice miso which is usually a lighter brown, soybean miso which is a yellowish colour and various light-coloured brown, almost beige misos which tend to be younger or aged for a shorter time.

Nutritionally, miso contains approximately 13% protein and 13% salt, as well as Vitamin A, niacin, calcium, phosphorus, potassium, iron and lecithin. Generally, miso is used like a bouillon in soups and stews, in sauces, dips and in dressings. One may also find miso in spreads, chutney and even as a pickling medium. Very little miso is needed for flavouring — usually 1/2 teaspoon per 1 cup of liquid.

Miso Daikon Soup (4 servings)

Miso soup is often served as a first course. It prepares the digestive system to receive the rest of the food and is very strengthening. Served this way, the number of vegetables is usually kept to two or three with a garnish.

one 2" strip of wakame
4 slices of daikon, fresh and sliced diagonally 1/2" thick and then into triangular-shaped pieces
2 scallions chopped finely, including stem
fresh kale or greens, chopped as a garnish
3-4 cups water or stock, including soaking water of wakame
1 small carrot sliced thinly on the diagonal

Soak wakame in 1/2 cup of the water or stock. Let soak five minutes and then chop into bite-sized pieces. Simmer gently in the total amount of stock for 15 minutes. Add sliced daikon and carrot and cook until tender. Purée 2 tsp. of miso, (barley or brown rice miso) in 1/2 cup of the hot soup and return purée to pot. Add scallions and kale and barely simmer 2-3 minutes. Serve hot. Variations: Add left over grain, cooked pasta — whole grain spirals, noodles, etc. for a heartier North American-style soup. Miso soup with pasta is especially popular with children.

Miso Soup with Barley
and Shitake Mushrooms (4 servings)

An all time favourite, the sweetness of the mushrooms blends superbly with the barley to make a hearty, toe-warming feast which is almost a meal in itself. Shitake mushrooms give a special sweet taste to this soup but regular mushrooms may be substituted and added near the end of cooking.

3/4 cups barley
6 cups spring water or vegetable stock
2 small onions
1 carrot
1/4 turnip or rutabaga
3-4 shitake mushrooms, dried or 8 regular fresh mushrooms

one 3 inch strip of wakame
2-3 tsp. of barley miso

Wash barley and cook in a pressure cooker with 3 cups of the water or stock for 40 minutes. Wash vegetables and cut onions into half moons. Cut all the other vegetables into one inch cubes. Soak wakame and shitake until soft. Add all ingredients to cooked barley and simmer 20-30 minutes until the vegetables are to your liking. Purée miso in 1/2 cup of the soup and add to the rest. Simmer 2-3 minutes. Garnish with parsley or greens and serve hot. 1/4-1/2 cup lentils may be added for variety.

Claude's Soup (serves 4)

This soup is especially popular with children, perhaps because of its sweet taste.

4 cups water or stock
2" piece of wakame
1 medium parsnip
1 large carrot
1 medium onion, diced
Greens such as kale or collard for garnish

Soak the wakame 5 minutes until soft. Chop into fine pieces and combine with 4 cups of water or stock. Bring to a boil and simmer 15 minutes. Slice the parsnip and carrot into thin diagonals. Add to the stock together with the diced onion. Simmer gently until the vegetables are tender, adding more water if necessary. Remove 1/3 cup of the liquid and add 2-2 1/2 tsp. barley miso. Stir miso in cup until completely dissolved. Return to soup and lower heat to minimum. Do not boil at this point as this will destroy the enzymes. Add finely chopped greens and serve hot.

Squash Soup Deluxe (4 servings)

1/2 cup azuki beans
4" strip dried kombu
1/4 medium squash
1 small onion, diced
several stalks of broccoli, greens, etc.

Soak azuki beans 5-6 hours with the kombu. Cut soaked kombu into small pieces and cook with beans until azukis are done. Dice squash into small pieces and add to beans. Dice onion and stalks and combine with 4-5 cups water (including juice from beans) in a soup pot. Cook all together until squash is soft. Add miso to taste (1/2 to 1 tsp. per cup liquid.) Serve hot with finely chopped greens or parsley.

Chickpea Soup (4-6 servings)

Chickpeas, also known as garbanzos, are high in protein and fibre and a source of calcium, iron, potassium, niacin and zinc. This soup is very satisfying on a cold or damp day or when you need a little comforting. The chickpeas must be soaked overnight or at least 6-8 hours and cooked very well for a considerably long period of time. Regular cooking requires 4 cups of water per cup of peas and 2-3 hours cooking time. Pressure cooking uses 2 1/2-3 cups of water per cup of chickpeas and 60 minutes cooking. The kombu aids in the digestion of the beans. It should be chopped into fine strips or pieces.

1 cup chickpeas, soaked 6-8 hours with 1 strip kombu, 6-8 inches long
1 small onion, diced
1 large carrot, diced
rice or barley miso to taste, 1-2 tsp.
3-4 cups water or vegetable stock
left over grain or a mochi cube
small clove of garlic, diced (optional)

Cook the chickpeas with the kombu as per above. Add the remaining 3-4 cups of water and the left over grain to the cooked garbanzos and cook another 20-30 minutes until the grain breaks down and the soup has a smooth, creamy texture. Dice the vegetables and add together with finely chopped garlic and cook in an open pot until the vegetables are tender. If using mochi, add with the vegetables. Purée the miso with 1/3 cup of hot soup, return to pot and turn heat down immediately. Garnish with parsley, celery leaves or finely chopped greens.

Creamy Carrot Soup (serves 4)

4 medium carrots
1 medium yellow onion
3-4 cups water or vegetable stock
1-2 tsp. miso, any kind
1/2 tsp. sesame or safflower oil
parsley sprigs or carrot tops

Scrub carrots, slice into small pieces. Place in a pressure cooker with 3 cups water and a pinch of salt. Pressure cook for 15-20 minutes. Slice onions into crescent moons and sauté in oil until translucent. Put everything into a blender and process until creamy. Return to heat adding more water to attain desired consistency (soup will thicken as it cools). You may wish to add 1-2 tbsp. kuzu or arrowroot diluted in 1/4 cup water or stock. Add 1-2 tsp. miso. Serve hot or cold, garnished with finely chopped parsley or carrot tops. Variations: carrots and squash, parsnips and onions, celery and onions, leeks and onions, etc.

Tofu, Tempeh,
Beans and a Fish

Tofu

Tofu originated in China and was later introduced to Japan. It is made from soya milk which has been coagulated with nigari, calcium sulfate, calcium chloride or magnesium chloride. Tofu made with either of the calcium-based coagulants will have a higher degree of calcium in the finished product.

Tofu contains a great deal of lysine, one of the essential amino acids in protein and therefore complements grains very well which are themselves deficient in this particular nutrient. Tofu is highly digestible — 95% compared to 68% for cooked soybeans and eight ounces contains only 147 calories and 11.5 grams of usable protein which is approximately 27% of an adult male requirement.

Soybean curd (another name for tofu) can have a cooling effect and as such it makes a very good summer dish. Generally it is not recommended as a dessert base but as an occasional treat (especially for dairy allergies), nothing beats a dish of freshly churned tofu ice cream.

Try to buy your tofu the same day you wish to use it and as fresh as possible. It can be kept in the fridge submerged in cold water. If the water is changed daily, tofu can keep up to 10 days.

Draining before using will help preserve the flavour and allows it to absorb sauces and seasoning more easily. Place the pieces on a flat surface and slant so that the water drains to one end or put in a colander and place over a bowl in the fridge. Drained tofu can be kept covered in the refrigerator for about twelve hours.

In general, tofu is served cubed in soups, stir frys, and stews, as an appetizer, or sliced and baked. It can be scrambled as are eggs or mashed and blended to make sauces or desserts.

One cake per person is plenty.

For more information about tofu, see *The Book of Tofu* by Shurtleff and Aoyagi, Ballantine Books.

Marinated Tofu and Vegetables on Noodles (4 people)

8-12 ounces of tofu, pressed
1/2 cup tamari
1/2 cup water
1 tsp. grated ginger, squeezed
1/4 small squash
1 bunch broccoli
2 small carrots
pasta for four

Cut pressed tofu into bite-size cubes. Marinate for several hours in mixture of tamari, water and ginger. Slice vegetables into medium sized pieces. Steam them together with the marinated tofu until vegetables are tender. Squash and carrots go on the bottom; broccoli and tofu on top. Prepare enough pasta for four people. Set aside. Serve vegetables over pasta using leftover marinade from the tofu as a sauce. Toasted sesame, sunflower or pumpkin seeds may be added as a garnish.

Tofu Mayonnaise (1 1/2 cups)

1/4 cup tofu
1-2 tbsp. lemon juice or mild vinegar
1 tsp. Dijon prepared mustard or 2 pinches dry mustard
1/2 tsp. tamari or 1/2 tsp. miso or 1/4 tsp. salt
1 tbsp. sunflower oil

Combine first four ingredients in a blender at lowest speed. When creamy, blend on higher speed and slowly pour oil into the mixture. Continue blending until thoroughly combined. Store in refrigerator for 2-3 days and use as you would commercial mayonnaise or add herbs, nuts or spices for a vegetable dip or salad dressing.

Tofu Ice Cream see Dessert Section

Barbecued Tofu

Two square blocks of tofu, pressed between 2 plates for one half hour or wrapped in several layers of paper towel to remove moisture. (One square block = 4 ounces).

Teriyaki Sauce

1/4 c. tamari
1 tbsp. mirin or sake or barley malt
3 pinches of dried mustard
1 pinch of horse radish
1 clove garlic, crushed or chopped finely
1/2 tsp. ground ginger and juice
1/2 tbsp. sesame oil
1/8 cup vegetable stock or water

Prepare marinade in order given. Slice tofu into 4 square pieces about 1/4" thick. Pour marinade over sliced tofu and marinate 1-2 hours. Grill, broil or brown in a skillet on top of the stove. (Latter method requires 1 tsp. sesame or vegetable oil). Tofu is done when nicely browned and of an egg-like texture. Serve in a bun with trimmings or over brown rice or whole wheat pasta with vegetables. For barbecue purposes you may wish to use thicker slices — 1/2 a 4 ounce cake or cubes skewered shish kebab style.

Scrambled Tofu

An excellent breakfast/brunch dish or quick snack.

2 cakes tofu (4 oz. each) pressed for 10 minutes
2-3 green onions, chopped
1 tsp. sesame oil

Sauté onions briefly in a skillet in the sesame oil. Add crumbled tofu and cook as for scrambled eggs. Serve with steamed matchstick carrots and broccoli or your favourite vegetables.

Baked Tofu and Natto Miso

2 four oz. cakes tofu, pressed
2 tbsp. natto miso and water to make a spreadable paste

Brush a cookie sheet with sesame oil. Slice pressed tofu into 1/4" thick pieces and lay flat on sheet. Spread paste on top of tofu. Don't use too much as natto miso is very rich. Bake at 400⁰ for 15 minutes to 1/2 hour. Barley or soybean miso may be used in the same way. Add 1 tsp. barley or rice malt, 1/2 tsp. squeezed ginger and 1 tsp chopped, soaked kombu.

Tofu Burgers (makes twelve 3" patties)

2 lbs. tofu, mashed (not necessary to press)
2 cups whole grain bread crumbs, fine
1 tbsp. tamari
1 clove garlic mashed to taste
1/2 cup celery, chopped finely
1/4 cup onion, chopped finely

Combine above ingredients. Form into 3" patties. Roll in 1/2 cup cornmeal and 1/4 cup flour mixed together. Sauté in oil on top of stove or grill or barbecue. Serve on a bun or bread or with grain and vegetables. For variation, add 1-2 tbsp. of almond, cashew or peanut butter.

Baked Tofu with Miso/Tahini Sauce

2 four oz. cakes tofu, cut into 1/4" slices and previously pressed
1 tbsp. miso (barley, rice or soya)
3 tsp. lemon juice
1/2 cup water or less
1 tbsp. rosted sesame seeds
2 tbsp. scallions
1 tsp. sesame tahini

This is a great way to serve tofu to a first time taster. The baked result has a cheese-like texture similar to ricotta.

Stack slices of tofu on end in a shallow baking dish so they are slightly tilted and lean on one another. Blend miso, lemon juice and sesame tahini together. Add enough water to

make a creamy sauce. Spoon sauce over tofu and bake at 350⁰
for 20 minutes. Garnish with scallions and freshly roasted
sesame seeds.

Fish in a bed of Greens (Serves four)

1 lb. white meat fish (sole, haddock, cod, hake, etc.)
3 tbsp. tamari soy sauce
1 tbsp. ginger
4 tbsp. water or 1 tbsp. mirin and 3 tbsp. water
5 cups sliced greens (kale, collard, chinese cabbage, etc.) — the
greener the better

Cut fish into chunks or small slices and marinate 15-30 minutes
in tamari, ginger and water (and mirin, if desired). Wash and
slice greens. Place them in the bottom of a large frying pan or
fairly shallow pot. Add fish and marinating sauce on top.
Cover and cook for 5-10 minutes or until fish is flaky. For
variety marinate cubes of tofu and steam with the fish.

Beans

Beans are a highly nutritious, often neglected source of
protein. They adapt themselves readily to casseroles, stews,
burgers, tortillas and baking, jumping right in to fill up the
space vacated by meat.

Bean Stew (serves 4)

1 cup kidney, pinto, navy or cattle beans (or your favourite)
(lentils can be used but require less cooking and taste much
better the next day)
2" strip kombu, soaked and cut into small pieces

Soak beans overnight according to the table on p. 68. Cook
required length of time and set aside or simmer longer at a very
low heat for increased flavour. Beans and stews taste sweeter if

cooked slowly with the occasional addition of cold water.

1 large onion, sliced or cubed
1 tsp. sesame oil
your choice of root vegetables — carrots, parsnips, turnips "chunked" or cubed
other vegetables as desired — squash, broccoli stems and tops, potatoes (optional)
tamari to taste

Sauté onion in the sesame oil. Add vegetables and sauté 5-10 minutes. Add cooked beans and sauce and more vegetable stock or water if necessary. Cook the stew slowly until vegetables are just tender. Some vegetables may be added later than others depending on cooking times. Add tamari and let sit several hours. Serve hot over rice or as a sauce for pasta.

Lentil Casserole (serves 6-10)

3 cups lentils, cooked and puréed
1 cup turnips, diced
1 cup squash, diced
2 onions, diced
1 egg (optional)
2 tsp. oil
2 tsp. tamari
1/2 cup water or vegetable stock

Sauté onions, turnips and squash in oil in open pressure cooker for 10 minutes. Add 1/2 cup water, cover and pressure-cook for 20 minutes. Mash with a fork and combine with remaining ingredients in a casserole pot. If not using pressure, cook vegetables on top of the stove until mashable. Bake casserole in a 350⁰ oven for approximately 30 minutes.

Chickpeas with carrots and kombu

1 cup chickpeas, soaked 6-8 hours in 3 cups water or stock
1 cup onions, diced
1 cup carrots, diced
1 strip kombu, 6-8 inches long, soaked and diced
pinch sea salt
3 cups water or vegetable stock

Place kombu and beans in a pressure cooker. Add soaking water and bring to pressure. Cook 15-20 minutes. Release pressure. Add onions and carrots and bring to a boil. Cover with lid (not pressure) and simmer 1 1/2 to 2 hours. Add tamari and continue cooking until beans are well done and most of liquid evaporated. If not using pressure, use 4 cups water and cook 2-3 hours on low heat. This recipe can be made into a delicious chickpea soup by adding more water, a clove of garlic, finely diced, left over grain (blenderize and add as thickener) and using barley or soya miso instead of tamari.

Adel's Egyptian Kusherie

This recipe comes from an Egyptian friend and is often daily fare in his home country. It is very inexpensive and delicious for large groups. The following is for four people. You can double and triple it accordingly.

Salad

1 medium cucumber
1 green pepper
2 medium tomatoes
2 stalks celery
2 carrots
1/2 bunch parsley or your favourite fresh herbs (optional)
1/2 head lettuce, shredded

Chop vegetables into uniform bite-size pieces. Combine in a large bowl. This part can be prepared in advance and stored covered, in the fridge.

Lentils and Rice

2 cups uncooked rice, short grain brown
2 cups uncooked green lentils

Bring lentils and rice to a boil in 4 cups of water. Cover, reduce heat and simmer until done.

Onions

Make plenty of onions as these are usually the star performers. Finely chop (don't grate) 6 or more medium to large onions. Fry the onions in approximately 4 ounces of oil (about 1/2 cup). When they are lightly browned, remove from heat and drain on paper towelling to soak up excess fat. Set aside.

Dressing

4 tbsp. reserved oil from onions (use same saucepan and all)
2-3 cloves of garlic, finely chopped (Egyptians used to pay their workers in onions and garlic which were considered to be the reigning monarchs of the vegetable world).
salt to taste
1/4 cup water
2-3 tbsp. vinegar
1 small can of tomato sauce — 7 oz.
1 scant tsp. cumin
Dash of chili powder or 2-3 drops of tabasco sauce

Discard extra oil, leaving just 4 tbsp. in the onion saucepan. Fry chopped garlic in the oil until lightly browned. Carefully add tomato sauce and water. Stir until well-blended. Bring to boil until slightly thickened (about 5 minutes). Add cumin, salt and chili. Lower heat and simmer for 10 minutes. Add vinegar and continue to simmer for a further 3 minutes.

Alternate non-tomato dressing

4 tbsp. reserved oil from onions
2-3 cloves of garlic, finely chopped
salt to taste
1/4 cup water
2-3 tbsp. vinegar or lemon
1 tsp. dried mustard

1 tsp. tarragon or 2/3 tsp. basil and 1/3 tsp oregano

Combine in order given. Shake well.

Serve the Kusherie in layers. Cover the plate first with rice and lentils mixture. Add a layer of cooked onions. Salad is heaped on top and dressing added last. Enjoy!

Bean Tortillas (serves 6)

1 cup azuki beans, uncooked
2" strip kombu, soaked 10 minutes
1/2 cup diced carrots
1 small onion diced
1 cup cooked rice or other grain
1 cup sauerkraut, rinsed
1 dozen corn tortillas

Soak azuki beans (or any other beans) overnight in 4 cups water for top-of-the stove cooking or 2 1/2-3 cups water if you pressure cook. Cook 40-50 minutes or 30 minutes in a pressure cooker. Mash slightly. Sauté the onions and carrots in sesame oil and combine with the cooked grain and mashed beans. Add tamari to taste. Steam tortillas in a strainer over boiling water and fill them with the beans, grain, vegetables and sauerkraut. Mustard or other condiments may be added for extra flavour.

Kidney Beans with Mustard (serves 4)

1 cup kidney beans, uncooked
3" strip of kombu
celery, carrots and onion, chopped in medium small pieces

Soak beans and kombu overnight. Cook according to table p 68. Steam vegetables (approx. 1-1 1/2 cups total) separately, or sauté them lightly in the oil of your choice. Add water and steam until soft. Add steamed vegetables to cooked beans and heat thoroughly together. Mix in 1 tsp. to 1 tbsp. Dijon prepared mustard to taste.

Aduki Beans with Kombu and Squash

(serves 4)

1 cup aduki beans, soaked overnight in two cups water
2 cups winter squash — buttercup, butternut, acorn
one 6 inch strip soaked kombu
sea salt or tamari

Soak kombu 10 minutes or until soft. Place on bottom of pot and place washed aduki beans on top. (Before washing, place on a flat plate and sort out any stones or foreign objects). Soak kombu and beans 6-8 hours or overnight in enough water to cover the beans. Include the kombu soaking water. In morning, cook uncovered for 15 minutes removing any foam that may rise to the surface. Cook covered until 80% done, adding more cold water as needed. When thoroughly cooked, a bean split in half will be totally white and slightly mushy. Chop the squash into bite-sized pieces or thin slices and place on top of the beans. Continue cooking the two, until squash is soft. Add a few drops of tamari or sea salt just before the end of cooking.

Baked Beans

This is a no-fail ever-popular recipe which we do in a large cast iron Dutch oven, but which lends itself to any type of ovenware.

Beans

2 cups white navy beans and 1 cup pintos
    or
1 cup navy beans, 1 cup pintos or cattle and 1 cup kidney beans

Soak beans separately overnight with a 1" strip of kombu for each kind. Pressure cook pintos and kidneys for 10 minutes. Run cold water over cooker to bring down the pressure. Add navy beans and pressure cook for another 10 minutes. (Double the cooking time for non-pressure.)

Sauce

1 med. onion, sliced or diced

1 tsp. sesame oil
4 oz. sweet and sour tempeh (see p. 70)
3 healthy tablespoons barley malt
1 tsp. powdered mustard
1 tbsp ume vinegar or 1 umeboshi plum mashed (optional)
1 tsp. brown rice or apple cider vinegar
1 tsp. grated ginger
prepared Dijon mustard (optional)

Sauté the onion in the teaspoon of sesame oil. Add 1/2 cup of the bean stock plus above ingredients and pour over beans in oven-proof dish. Bake 4-5 hours at 250⁰ or until beans start to absorb the sauce and turn brown. When beans are 3/4 done, add sweet and sour tempeh* and cook for approximately one hour longer. Adjust seasoning, adding some prepared Dijon mustard or hot Eden prepared mustard for an extra zing. Baked beans taste better the next day so let them sit a while before serving.

* See p. 70 for sweet 'n sour recipe.

Split Yellow Peas (Serves 4-6)

Split peas and beans are not really a whole food and are comparable to split grains such as bulgur and cous cous. They are very delicious in soups and casserole-type dishes and are good for variety.

8 oz. yellow split peas (225 gm)
1 pint (550 ml) water
2 medium onions, peeled and sliced
1 medium carrot, sliced on the diagonal
1 small leek, cleaned and sliced medium thinly
1 celery, sliced medium
pinch of dried mint or marjoram (up to 1 tsp. depending on taste)
1 tsp. lemon juice (optional)
sea salt
sesame oil for sautéing

Soak split peas in water for an hour or two. Drain and rinse

Cooking Dry Beans

Beans (1 cup dry)	Soaking Time	Non-Pressure water time (cups)		Pressure Cooking water time (cups)	
Azuki	unsoaked	4	90 min.	2 1/2-3	45 min.
	1 hour	4	60 min.	2 1/2-3	30 min.
Black	overnight	4	2-3 hrs.	2 1/2-3	60 min.*
Chick-peas	overnight	4	2-3 hrs.	2 1/2-3	60 min.
Kidneys	unsoaked	3	90 min.	2 1/2	60 min.
	1 hr.	3	60 min.	2 1/2	45 min.
Lentils	unsoaked	3	60-90	2 1/2	30 min.
	1 hr.	3	45	2 1/2	25 min.
Navy beans	unsoaked	3	90 min.	2 1/2	50 min.
	1 hr.	3	60 min.	2 1/2	40 min.
Pintos	unsoaked or overnight soaked	3	2-2 1/2 hr.	2 1/2-3	60 min.
Soybeans	overnight	4	3 hrs.	2 1/2-3	90 min.*
Split peas	unsoaked	3	45 min.	2 1/2	20 min.

Alternative to overnight soaking: Bring beans and water to a boil. Cover and remove from stove. Let sit 1 hour and then cook by method of your choice.

Seasoning:
pinch of sea salt per cup of dry beans — add at end of cooking if not using kombu
addition of oil — at end when soft
tamari sauce — add to taste during last 5 minutes of cooking

Yield: 1 cup dry beans makes about 2 1/2 cups cooked

Vegetables and seaweed: Vegetables should be added in diced or finely cut form during the last 1/2 hour of cooking. If pressure cooking, add vegetables after pressure has come down and continue cooking until vegetables are soft. Kombu should be added for flavour and minerals. It also cuts down on foaming and aids in digestion. When pressure cooking bring to a boil first and skim off any foam that may arise before covering and bringing to pressure. Millet or wheat berries may be added for up to 1/4 of the azuki beans. Wheat berries require additional cooking time.

and place in a saucepan with 1 pint water, 1/2 total onion and all the other vegetables and herbs. Simmer gently until peas are soft and vegetables tender, approximately 30 minutes. Mash up in a suribachi or blender until purée consistency. Add lemon juice, salt or tamari. Place in a heat-proof dish. Fry remaining onion until soft and place on top of purée. Put under broiler and brown until top is slightly crusted and onion crisp and brown. Split peas lend themselves well to soups. Use onions, carrots and celery, diced and add a bit of miso for flavour instead of tamari. Puréeing is not necessary for soup.

Tempeh

Tempeh may seem a bit exotic to the neophyte but once tasted, twice hooked. It usually comes in a solid cake and is essentially just yellow soybeans, sometimes in combination with grain or other beans, that have been cooked and fermented. Often you will find a grey/blackish mold on top. This is quite normal. Tempeh can be kept in the refrigerator for about a week and can be frozen for considerably longer periods of time. It is of Indonesian origin and is a good source of vitamin B_{12} which is essential to vegetarians. Please refer to *The Book of Tempeh* by William and Akiko Shurtleff, Harper and Row, 1979.

The following recipes are favourites, but generally tempeh can be used in sandwiches, burgers, patés, baked beans and kebobs for barbecues or anyway you would use meat. It must always be cooked and is not recommended to eat raw.

Tempeh Extraordinaire (Serves 4)

This recipe produces a crispy, crunchy tempeh which resembles bacon.

4 oz. tempeh, millet/soybean is the most crispy
2 tsp. sesame oil

Slice tempeh in thin pieces. Fry slices on both sides in hot oil until brown and crispy. Use as you would bacon or serve as a meat substitute with vegetables and rice.

Sweet and Sour Tempeh (4-6 servings)

8 oz. tempeh
sesame or safflower oil for sautéing — 1-2 tsp.
1/4 cup umeboshi vinegar or brown rice or apple cider vinegar
1/4 cup cooking sherry or mirin
1/4 cup water

Slice the block of tempeh in half and then into thirds lengthwise. Slice each of the six thirds into three thin slices. Heat the oil and brown the tempeh on both sides. Add the water/mirin/vinegar mixture and simmer 20 minutes until tender and tantalizing. Serve with vegetables or add to baked beans.

Tempeh Stew

8 oz. tempeh, cut into small chunks
2 carrots, sliced fairly thick (1/4")
1/2 medium-sized turnip in 1/2" slices
1 onion, medium slices
1 small potato (optional)
1 cup broccoli, flowerets and stems sliced into thick rounds
1/2 cup cauliflower

Sauté tempeh in 1 tsp. sesame oil. Sauté onions and other vegetables in oil or water. Add vegetable stock or water and cook for about 20-30 minutes until tender. Season with tamari or umeboshi plum diluted with water or brown rice vinegar, tamari and water. Cook another 5 minutes. Pour over noodles or rice and serve hot.

Tempeh Reuben

Delightful as a sandwich or with rice and vegetables.

8 oz. tempeh, sliced thinly
1/4 cup tamari
1/4 cup vegetable stock or water
dash grated ginger
prepared Dijon mustard to taste
1/2 cup sauerkraut

Mix tamari, water and ginger. Marinate tempeh in this mixture for 10-15 minutes. Remove tempeh from liquid and place on a flat cookie sheet. Brush with prepared mustard and place in 350⁰ oven 10-15 minutes until browned or brush a skillet with oil and sauté tempeh until done. Serve with sauerkraut adding more mustard if desired.

Sea Vegetables

Sea Vegetables

The most often used and most commonly known sea vegetables are arame, hijiki, dulse, nori, wakame and kombu. These are for the most part Japanese in origin. Similar varieties are harvested on the East and West coasts of North America. All of the above-mentioned are available in any good health food store or in specialty outlets catering to Korean or Oriental tastes. Sea vegetables are a new and exciting source of minerals and vitamins that may take some getting used to but promise to be an adventure in gourmet dining.

Arame

This delicate specimen from the sea is found dried in wirey, black, spider-like meshes. To avoid a fishy taste, it should always be washed thoroughly by swirling about in a bowl and the soaking water should be thrown out and replaced by clean cooking water. Adding rice vinegar, lemon juice or umeboshi plum chemically breaks down the cells of the seaweed and releases the minerals and flavours more completely. Arame is a rich source of calcium, iron, phosphorus, iodine and potassium.

Arame for beginners (serves 4)

1/3 cup dried arame
1 carrot sliced thinly on the diagonal or in matchsticks
1/2 onion sliced thinly in crescent-shaped moons
1/2 cup green wax beans or green peas
1/2-1 tsp. grated fresh ginger

1 tsp. rice malt or honey

Wash the arame very carefully by swishing about in a small bowl. Soak washed arame 10-15 minutes until soft and expanded. Chop up into 1-2" lengths. Cover with fresh water and simmer in a frying pan or small pot for 15 minutes. Discard cooking water and set aside cooked arame. Sauté onions in 1 tsp. sesame oil or water until translucent. Put in carrots and green beans. Sauté briefly. Add 2-3 tbsp. water and simmer vegetables until almost tender. Add ginger, rice malt and a splash of tamari. Place arame on top, with more water if necessary. Simmer five more minutes or until vegetables are cooked to your liking. Mix up everything and serve warm. Tahini may be substituted for the malt and ginger and parsnips or any sweet root vegetable can be used with onions, instead of the green beans and peas. Vinegar or lemon juice may be added during the first cooking of the arame.

Arame for Connoisseurs

This recipe combines two unusual vegetables — arame and lotus root. The two contrasting textures of crunchy and soft produce a very tasty experience.

1 small handful of dried arame or hijiki
4 pieces of dried or fresh lotus
1 small onion

Wash off lotus root and if dried, soak several hours or overnight. Throw away the soaking water and cut each piece in half on the length (if thick) and then into four or five smaller pieces. Boil in 1/2 cup water for 1-2 hours. Fresh lotus can be prepared along with the onion without pre-soaking. Wash and soak and cook arame as per above recipe. Set aside. Sauté onion in 1/2 tsp. sesame oil. Add the lotus root and sauté two more minutes. Place arame on top, adding 2-4 tbsp. water and a touch of tamari. Steam 10-15 minutes.

Note:
Lotus root can be purchased dried in Chinese Specialty shops. It is considered to be very beneficial for lung-related diseases and in eliminating mucus from the body. The lacy pattern of

the lotus root resembles the construction of the lungs with a delicate "breathing" via the tiny, interconnected spaces.

Hijiki

This wonderful sea vegetable is really the king of the sea. It ressembles arame but is thicker and more rope-like. Hijiki will quadruple in size so a small amount dried goes a long way. One quarter cup of cooked hijiki contains 152.6 mg calcium and 3.16 mg of iron. It also contains large quantities of Vitamins A, B_1, B_2 and phosphorus. Hijiki should be prepared like arame and can be substituted for arame in most recipes. It has a stronger, more substantial taste than arame. Don't forget to cut hijiki after soaking or you will end up with black spaghetti.

Hijiki à l'orange (serves 4)

1/2 cup hijiki, dried
2 medium carrots, sliced 1/4" thick on the diagonal
1/2 onion sliced thinly
2-3 shitake mushrooms, soaked (optional)

Wash hijiki carefully to remove stones and dirt. Soak 20 minutes or until soft. Throw out soaking water. Chop into 2" lengths or cut with scissors. Simmer 20 minutes in 1/2-1 cup fresh water. Drain. Sauté onions in 1 tsp. sesame oil or 2 tsp. water. Slice shitake mushrooms into tiny pieces. Keep the soaking water. Add them together with carrots to the onions and sauté two minutes longer. Add three to four tablespoons of soaking water from the mushrooms and simmer until the vegetables are tender. Place the hijiki on top with a drop or two of tamari and more liquid if necessary. Simmer 5-10 minutes. Shitake mushrooms give a special sweetness to any dish. A drop or two of rice malt or honey may be used in place of the mushrooms.

Hijiki-Tofu Delight

1/2 cup hijiki
1 tbsp. tahini

1/2 tsp. umeboshi paste or 1 tsp. brown rice or umeboshi vinegar

4 ozs. tofu

roasted sunflower or pumpkin seeds

Soak washed hijiki for 15-20 minutes, chop lightly and simmer for 30 minutes or until soft. (Pressure cooking for 10 minutes will give an interesting taste and texture). Combine tahini, umeboshi paste and tofu in a sauce pan with 1/2 cup water and simmer for 5 minutes. Blend in blender or suribachi until creamy. Pour over hijiki and top with roasted seeds. Serve cool for summer or warm for winter.

Hijiki Rolls

These are a real party stopper and are absolutely scrumptious!

2 cups cooked hijiki and finely chopped vegetables (carrots, onions, etc.)

1 large pie crust, wholewheat

Prepare a pie crust — see lemon pie, p. 116. Roll out as for a pie shell. Prepare hijiki and vegetables. Drain thoroughly and cool. Spread mixture evenly on the crust, leaving about 1" on either side uncovered. Roll up, seal the edges with water as in making strudel. Bake at 350⁰ for 30-35 minutes. Cool and slice into one inch rounds as for sushi. Serve so as to expose the hijiki as a spiral in the middle.

Nori

Nori is a lavender seaweed in the water and dries to a dark purple or black that turns bright green when toasted. It is most often purchased in rectangular sheets and usually must be toasted before use. This can be done very easily by holding the untoasted piece by two corners and passing quickly over a flame on a gas stove or an electric element until a bright green colour appears when held up to the light. Sheets of nori can then be divided into four and consumed with meals or shredded and eaten on top of rice or vegetables or in soups. Nori contains a lot of calcium, potassium, manganese, magnesium and phosphorus. It is also a good source of Vitamin A, Niacin and Vitamin C.

Nori Balls

Nori is used in making sushi, the famous Japanese appetizer. The following recipe is like sushi but considerably less work. These are excellent travel companions and are very soothing to the stomach. They can also be eaten with a hearty soup for lunch at home.

1-2 cups cooked brown rice
4-5 umeboshi plums with pits
3-4 sheets toasted nori, divided into quarters
small bowl of water

Wet your hands thoroughly and make a ball of brown rice large enough to fit between your two palms. Poke a hole in one side and insert an umeboshi plum or piece of plum (depending on how large the ball turns out to be). Reshape the ball so as to close up the hole. Take a quarter piece of nori and cover one side of the rice ball. Continue to cover with nori until there is no rice visible. Use a tiny bit of water to seal the nori well. Wrap in waxed paper and store in a cool, dry place such as a cupboard or pantry. Do not refrigerate, as the nori will become too moist. Rice balls usually keep up to three days without refrigeration, depending on the weather. Variations include using other grains alone or in combination with brown rice.

Dulse

Dulse is no stranger to Maritimers. It grows well in the cold waters of both the Atlantic and Pacific Oceans. Dulse is eaten as a snack as is or used in salads, soups, stews and breads. (See corn meal muffins, p. 100). It is a deep purple colour and has the highest percentage of iron of any food. It is also very rich in calcium, iodine, potassium, magnesium and phosphorus. A friend showed me the following way to eat dulse as a snack. It's very addictive! Simply wrap a piece of dulse around a raw (or toasted) almond and munch away. A few pieces of apple or bread tucked into your bag of dulse will keep it moist and chewable.

Try shredding this sea vegetable into small pieces and adding to pressed or fresh salad. Or combine with grain or pasta and stir fry it with vegetables. The following makes a delightful summer salad or side dish.

Purple Rice Salad

2 cups cooked rice
1/2 medium cucumber, diced
2 small scallions, including stems, sliced finely
4-5 radishes or daikon, thin diagonals
3-4 small carrots, thin diagonals
6 strips of dulse, torn into small pieces (1-2 handfuls)
handful finely diced parsley or carrot tops
1-2 tbsp. olive oil
juice of 1/2 lemon or more

Cut up vegetables and place in a bowl. Add dulse and rice. Pour over olive oil. Mix thoroughly. Add the lemon juice and toss well. Eat!

Kombu

This sea vegetable is an essential part of Japanese cuisine. It is even made into a candy that resembles a licorice taffy in texture. Kombu is high in Vitamins A, B_2, C, calcium and iodine. To clean simply wipe off with a moist towel or brush. Do not scrub as the white flecks are important to taste and nutritive value. Soak 5-10 minutes before cutting and cooking, but don't leave too long in water as it becomes very slippery and hard to handle. Kombu is usually cooked with bean dishes. It aids in the digestion of legumes by breaking down the protein into a more easily assimilated nutrient.

Wakame

Wakame can be substituted in any recipe calling for kombu. Both are part of the Laminaria family which is harvested in Japan and on the Pacific and Atlantic Coasts. Alaria resembles wakame and is found off the coast of Maine. Wakame is very high in calcium, iron, Vitamins A & C, niacin and protein. It is used in making miso soup (p. 50) and salads, such as cucumber-wakame salad, p. 86 or with bean dishes in place of kombu.

Pickles

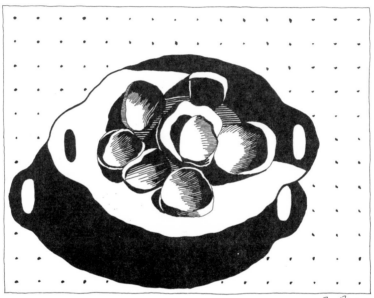

Pickles

Variety adds interest to any meal. Pickles add a unique taste that is very enriching texture-wise and very healthy digestion-wise. Try to include a small amount of sour vegetable in every meal.

Sauerkraut can be made at home but most communities tend to sell it at a very reasonable rate. The tastiest is usually the simplest that is made with just salt and cabbage. Sauerkraut can be served in small amounts as a side dish or combined with beans as a tortilla filling (see bean tortillas, p. 65).

Tamari Daikon Pickles

Daikon is a white radish often used in Chinese and Japanese cooking. It is highly praised for its ability to facilitate in the breaking up of fat in the body. Grated daikon is squeezed to remove excess water and then combined with a few drops of tamari. This is then served as a side dish when consuming fatty dishes such as tempura or fish.

Tamari daikon pickles don't take long to prepare and are a very tasty addition to any meal.

1 small daikon, about 5" long
1/2 cup tamari
1/2 cup water

Cut daikon into 1/4" slices on the diagonal. Cut each slice into matchstick pieces and marinate in a sauce of equal parts tamari and water, for an hour or two. Pour off the liquid before serving and use for cooking or once more as a marinade. Carrots or turnip may be used in place of daikon. The amount of liquid varies with the amount of vegetables. It should just cover the vegetables.

Pickled Ginger or Ginger Pickles

These can be purchased in most health food stores or Oriental places. They are a wonderful pink colour and have a hot, poignant taste. Do not pop one into your mouth — you will have a rude awakening. Try breaking them into small amounts and eating with rice, vegetables or noodles. Keep refrigerated after opening.

Pressed Pickles

Some health food stores carry a wonderful plastic invention called a pickle press. If you do not have such an ingenious device, use a plate with a weight in a large bowl or any contraption that will press down on the vegetables and help to extract the water. This recipe is very unusual tasting but is often a favourite with the most novice of whole food connoisseurs.

3 cups vegetables — Chinese cabbage, red radish, daikon, green onion, cucumber, celery, red onion, etc.
1 tsp. sea salt or 2 tbsp. umeboshi vinegar. (Umeboshi vinegar will give a very unique flavour and is a real favourite for this recipe. See the glossary for further information).

Wash and slice vegetables into very thin pieces and place into the pickle press or a bowl. Sprinkle with sea salt or vinegar and mix. Screw down top of press or use a bowl with a weighted plate. Leave about one hour and then drain off liquid. Vegetables should be slightly soft but not soggy. If the salad tastes too salty, rinse before serving.

Cucumber Wakame Salad

This is an all time favourite and very appealing colour-wise.

three 6 inch strips of wakame
1 small cucumber
6 red radishes
2 scallions
1/2 tsp. sea salt or 1 1/2 tbsp. umeboshi vinegar

Rinse wakame and place in a dish with water to cover. Let soak 1-2 minutes, cut into small pieces and cook in the soaking water for 5-10 minutes. Strain and set aside. Wash and slice vegetables into thin slices and place in a pickle press. Add salt and mix well, or sprinkle with umeboshi vinegar. Press for 30-45 minutes. Mix wakame into pressed salad and serve.

The following recipes come from Ann 'Blue Jay' Burns, a wonderful lady who lives in Brookline, Massachusetts.

Pickled Beets

2 small bunches beets, sliced thin
4 cups water
2 tsp. sea salt
2 cloves garlic, crushed (optional)
1/2 cup brown rice vinegar

Steam beets for 5 minutes and set aside. Bring water to a boil and add salt, garlic and vinegar. Set aside to cool. Pour cooled liquid over beets in a crock or jar and let sit, covered with a cloth or a bamboo mat, 3-5 days before serving. Store in refrigerator.

Red Cabbage Sauerkraut

1 head red cabbage, shredded
1/3 cup sea salt
1 1/2 tbsp. caraway seeds
1/2 cup brown rice vinegar

Place 1/3 of the cabbage in a crock. Sprinkle on 1/3 of the salt and 1/3 of the caraway seeds over the cabbage. Make two more layers, ending with salt and seeds. Pour the vinegar over all. Cover with a plate and place a weight of approximately 6 pounds on top (a large rock or a gallon jug of water works well). Cover with a clean cotton dish towel and let sit in a cool place at least three days. When the cabbage is pickled, rinse lightly in a strainer to remove some of the salt and store in the refrigerator.

Quick Dill Pickles

This is a marvellous, quick way to prepare dills.

6 cucumbers
1/2 purple onion
1 bunch fresh dill
1/2 cup water
1/2 cup apple cider vinegar
2 tsp. sea salt
1 tsp. garlic powder or 2 cloves mashed fresh

Peel and score cucumbers, and cut in 1/4" rounds. (Scoring creates little ridges that make a flower shape when the cucumber is sliced crosswise. With tines of a fork, scratch lengthwise of peeled cucumbers and then slice). Slice onion thinly, and chop dill. Toss vegetables together and place in a crock or jar. Combine water, vinegar, salt and garlic and pour over vegetables. Cover with a cloth and let stand for two hours before serving. Store the remainder in refrigerator. This is a refreshing summer/fall pickle that is almost like a marinated salad.

Grazia a Douglas, Halifax's most infamous Italian chef, for the following delicacies.

Marinated Zucchini

4 small zucchini
olive oil
2 bay leaves
1-2 cloves garlic
1/4 tsp. salt
1/4 tsp. oregano
vinegar
water

Slice zucchini into 1/4" pieces. Sauté until soft in olive or safflower oil. Place in a jar with a screw lid and add 2 bay leaves, minced garlic, salt and oregano. Cover with a mixture of equal parts vinegar to water. (Your choice of vinegar will determine the taste). Leave in refrigerator 24 hours to marinate. These will keep ten days to two weeks. Serve at room temperature for optimal flavour.

Marinated Cauliflower

1 medium cauliflower
green pepper or green peas
2 oz. olive oil
3 oz. vinegar, your choice
1/4 chopped fresh mint, or 2 tbsp. dried mint
1-2 cloves garlic, chopped

Divide cauliflower into bite-sized flowerettes. Wash and steam until tender (approximately 8 minutes). Slice green pepper into narrow strips and steam until just tender *or* steam green peas lightly for 2-3 minutes. Prepare a marinade of 2 oz. oil, 3 oz. vinegar, mint and garlic. Pour over vegetables in a shallow dish or bowl. Refrigerate 1 hour, stirring occasionally. These will keep several days in the refrigerator. They taste best served at room temperature.

Umeboshi Pickles

3-4 whole umeboshi plums
1-2 cups thinly sliced vegetables, such as radishes, carrots, broccoli, turnips, green onions, chinese cabbage, etc.
spring or tap water

Place plums in a jar and place vegetables on top of plums. Boil enough water to completely cover the vegetables and allow it to return to room temperature. Fill the jar with the cooled water and cover with cheesecloth, secured by a rubber band. Leave 3-5 days at cool room temperature, stirring each day. These will keep refrigerated about one week.

Bread
and Breakfast

Bread and Breakfast

Breakfast should be nourishing but not so heavy that you want to go back to bed. Following are some breakfast possibilities. For a more adventuresome approach to your first meal of the day, try leftover soup such as barley, cream of vegetable or miso with whole grain crackers, muffins or bread. These are especially warming on cold winter mornings.

Whole Grain Porridge (4 servings)

1 cup whole grain — oat groats, whole rye, wheat berries, rice, millet, barley
4-5 cups water
pinch sea salt

Wash grain. If using a pressure cooker, bring to pressure with 4-5 cups water. Lower heat and leave on lowest heat overnight or turn off heat and leave covered overnight on top of stove or in a warm oven. Whole grains may also be soaked overnight and pressure cooked with 4-5 cups water (including soaking water) for one hour in the morning. For non pressure method, bring water to a boil. Add grain. Place pot on a flame tamer on lowest heat and leave overnight or let sit covered as per above on top of the stove or in a warm oven. Serve with dried fruit and nuts or a dash of barley malt or maple syrup.

Cooked Flakes (4-6 servings)

2 cups flaked oats, wheat, rye, rice or soya beans (or a combination)
2 pinches salt
6 cups boiling water

Heat a large saucepan or frying pan. Place flakes in the hot pan and dry roast for about 5 minutes on a medium-low heat stirring constantly. Add boiling water and salt. Cover and cook on low heat for 20-30 minutes, stirring occasionally. Add raisins, chopped dried fruit, nuts, roasted sunflower and pumpkin seeds for variety.

Peanut Butter Oatmeal

Prepare oatmeal as usual (1 cup flakes to 3 cups water, or to the consistency you prefer). Add a tablespoon of peanut, almond or cashew butter to individual servings. A touch of soya milk makes for decadence at this point!

Cream of Rice (2-3 servings)

1 cup brown rice
5 cups water
pinch sea salt
umeboshi plum, 2-3 small pieces

Bring water to a boil. Add rice and boil 45-60 minutes until creamy. Pressure cook for the same length of time. Add umeboshi plum before serving for an extra gentle touch. This may also be simmered overnight on very low heat using 10 cups of water to 1 cup rice or you may wish to add some sweet rice, reducing the water by 1/4 to 1/2 to allow for the extra gluten.

Quick Porridge (2-3 servings)

1/4 cup buckwheat, uncooked
1/2 cup rice, cooked
handful dried apples
4 miniscule pieces of candied ginger or a suggestion of grated ginger
handful raisins
6 almonds or walnuts, roasted and cut into small pieces

Cook buckwheat in 1/2 cup of stock for 15 minutes (until water is absorbed). Add cooked rice and other ingredients and 1/2 tsp. of barley malt or yinnie. Delicious!

Granola (serves 4)

2 cups rolled oats
1 cup wheat flakes
1 cup flaked rye, wheat or rice (or a combination)
1/4 cup wheat or corn germ
1/4 cup bran
1/4 cup pumpkin seeds
1/4 cup sunflower seeds
1/2 cup chopped walnuts, almonds or filberts
1/4 cup safflower oil or corn oil
3 tbsp. barley malt mixed with 1/4 cup boiling water or 1/4 cup maple syrup
1 tsp. pure vanilla extract (optional)
3 good pinches of salt
raisins, currants or chopped, dried fruit

Preheat oven to 350^0. Measure the flakes, seeds and nuts into a large bowl. Heat oil, barley malt and boiling water in a large dutch oven. When thin, add vanilla and turn heat to very lowest. Add dry ingredients one cup at a time, mixing well in between. Lower oven to 300^0. Place granola on flat cookie sheet and bake twenty minutes, stirring often, until brown and crispy. Cool, add dried fruit and store in glass jars or an airtight container.

Cold Cereal with Soya or Nut Milk

1 bowl of puffed rice, wheat, corn or millet or granola
1/4 cup almonds
1/4 cup cashews
2 cups water
sweetener (optional)

Place almonds, cashews and 1 cup of water in a blender. Blend at medium speed, stopping occasionally, until creamy and thick. Add the rest of the water and sweetener and blend again to make a thick, milk-like consistency. Pour over cereal and indulge! Soymilk may also be used here. It can be purchased prepackaged in Health Food stores. Many oriental food stores carry large bags at a very low price. This soymilk often comes from the tofu makers who supply the store.

Sourdough Pancakes or Waffles

Sponge

sourdough starter
2 cups whole wheat flour, pastry or bread
1-2 cups water

Feed sourdough starter (see Bread Section) by adding 2 cups of whole wheat flour and enough water to make a thick batter. Let sit overnight. Remove 1 cup of the sponge in the morning and keep in the refrigerator as starter for next time.

Batter for pancakes

1 tbsp. barley malt or maple syrup
3 tbsp. corn oil
2 pinches sea salt
1 egg (optional)
1-2 cups buckwheat, rice, soya, corn flour with wholewheat (use a combination with 60% whole wheat)

Add above ingredients in order to the sponge, saving the flour for the end. Mix in enough additional water or juice to make a pourable batter. Cook on a hot, oiled grill and serve with fruit and rice or maple syrup. Fresh fruit such as apples or blueberries may be mixed in with the batter as well.

Scrambled Tofu

This makes a wonderful, light breakfast. Please see Tofu chapter.

Beverages

Most North Americans have a tendency to drink from habit rather than from thirst. Too many liquids can overwork the kidneys and weaken the body. Warm or hot drinks are much gentler and nurturing to our bodies. Cold food and drinks can shock the digestive system and the intestines.

Coffee Substitutes

There are many grain coffees available commercially. Most are made from barley and dandelion root. A drop of soya milk or barley malt gives a special taste.

Herbal Teas

Many herbal teas have specific medecinal uses and as such can lead to an imbalance through continuous use. They can be very soothing and satisfying but are best enjoyed on special occasions.

Kukicha Twig Tea

This tea is made from the stems and twigs of the same plant or bush used to make most black teas. It is harvested in the summer or fall when most of the caffeine has left the plant. Also known as bancha twig tea, kukicha is very good for the digestion and soothing to the stomach. A glass pyrex tea pot on a star-shaped, metal heat absorber works well for bancha. Place 2 scant tablespoons of twig tea in 1 1/2 quarts of cold water. Bring to a boil. Lower heat and simmer for 2-3 minutes. Strain and serve. Twigs may be re-used several times. Bancha is enjoyed by children and adults as is, with no added sweeteners or milk necessary.

Breads and Muffins

Generally speaking, flour products are pretty heavy to carry around. Inside the body they have a tendency to act as sponges. Remember what happens when you place a piece of bread in water. (If you don't, experiment). If eaten to excess, yeasted breads can cause bloating, indigestion and mucus conditions. Bread and muffins are very psychologically satisfying and make great treats for special occasions.

Any of your favourite recipes can be adapted by substituting barley or rice malt for the sweetener, using a sprinkling of yeast or sourdough starter instead of baking powder, warming the muffin tins for added rising power and using corn oil instead of butter or margarine. Soymilk, water or fruit juice can replace cow's milk.

Sourdough Starter

Sourdough starter is basically a form of yeast. It works the same as the store-bought product but tends to be more easily digested and is a purer form of leavening.

2 cups stone ground whole wheat flour
2 cups water

Place flour and water in a glass or ceramic bowl. Stir to form a thick porridge-like batter. Let sit at room temperature for 2-5 days, stirring daily with a wooden spoon. When the mixture smells sour, transfer to a small glass jar. Leave uncovered at room temperature for another day or two or until a sweet flavour develops. Pour off any dark liquid that may develop. Cover and store in refrigerator. Use for breads (in place of yeast), pancakes or muffins. Replenish the starter each time from a sponge or with dough after the first rising.

Sourdough Raisin Bread (makes 2 loaves)

Sourdough bread does not necessarily have a sour taste. After kneading, the dough is left to rise or it is proofed in baker terminology. Too high a temperature during proofing can cause an overly sour taste. Bread prepared in the morning and baked at night usually turns out better as does bread baked on sunny days and during the full moon.

1 batch of sourdough starter
2 cups water
5 cups stoneground wholewheat flour or a mixture of 60% wholewheat and 40% rye, corn flour, soya, barley, rice flours, cornmeal or unbleached white
1 tbsp. corn oil
1 tbsp. barley malt
1 tsp. sea salt

Take starter out of refrigerator and let it warm up for several hours or overnight. Add two cups of water and 2 1/2 cups of whole wheat flour. Cover with a bamboo mat or light cloth and leave in a warm place overnight. (The pilot light of a gas oven works well). Use a large ceramic or glass bowl for the sponge as it will expand. The sponge should resemble a thick yet pourable wallpaper paste. In the morning, set aside a jar of the sponge for next time's starter. Add enough flour to produce a solid mass that comes away from the sides of the bowl. Turn onto a floured surface and knead 300-350 times, adding whole wheat flour as you go until the dough holds together and springs back when touched. Knead in raisins or sunflower and sesame seeds and place in well-oiled loaf pans to rise. Oil tops with corn oil or warm water. Let rise 4-6 hours until loaves reach the tops of the pans. Cut through the top lengthwise with a sharp knife. Bake 1-2 hours at 300-350⁰ depending on the intensity of your oven. Bread is done when the crust turns brown and the loaf pulls away from the pan. The bottom should sound hollow when tapped. Cool upside down on racks approximately 20-30 minutes before loosening sides with a knife and removing from pan. Loaves may be oiled immediately upon removal from oven for a softer crust. Store in a paper bag in the open air.

Corn Meal Muffins (8 large, 12 small)

These muffins have no flour and are absolutely heavenly. They are very compact and one is a whole meal in itself. Serve with apple butter or fruit spread.

3 cups corn meal
1/4 tsp. salt
1/4 cup corn oil, scant
2 cups boiling water
1/2-3/4 cups cold water
1-2 tbsp. barley or rice malt (optional)
2 ears corn (optional)
3 tbsp. shredded dulse (omit salt) — optional

Boil water. Pour over corn meal and let sit 10 minutes. Mix salt, oil, corn and dulse. Add to corn meal and water and mix together quickly. Add enough cold water to make a thick yet pourable batter. Mix but don't overmix. Oil muffin tins and preheat by placing in a 250⁰ oven for 5-10 minutes. Bake at 350⁰ for 20-30 minutes. Let cool a few minutes and remove from pan.

Oatmeal Crackers (about 12-14)

These rarely last long. They are delicious with soup or for a snack.

1 cup water or soy milk
2 tbsp. barley or rice malt
1 tsp. salt or less
1/4-1/3 cup corn oil
3 cups rolled oats
1 cup whole wheat flour, stoneground or steel
1/4 cup sesame seeds (optional)

Mix in order given. Knead briefly. Roll out very thin between wax paper. Cut into squares or strips. Bake at 350⁰ for 15-25 minutes, depending on thickness. Delicious!

Carrot Bran Muffins

These wonderful creations come from Mrs. Murphy's Kitchen

in Halifax, whipped up by Mrs. Murphy herself. About 12 small muffins.

1/4 cup oil
3/4 cup barley malt
2 cups grated carrots
2 eggs
1/2 cup apple juice
1 cup whole wheat flour
2 teaspoons homemade baking powder (p. 106)
1/2 tsp. sea salt
1 tsp. cinnamon
2 tbsp. wheat germ
2 cups natural bran
1 cup raisins

Mix dry and wet ingredients separately. Combine the two with a few swift strokes. Do not overmix. Fill greased and floured muffin tins 3/4 full. Bake at 350⁰ for 30-35 minutes.

Dried Fruit Purée or Jam

1 pound dried apricots, figs, currants, peaches or prunes
2 cups strong mu tea or mint tea
1 cup apple cider
1/4 tsp. sea salt
1 bar agar-agar, washed and soaked in 1 cup apple juice for 30 minutes or 5 tbsp. agar flakes sprinkled in 1 cup apple juice
Grated lemon or orange rind
cinnamon, optional

Soak dried fruit in tea and cider overnight. In the morning, add salt and simmer in a covered saucepan for one hour. Purée fruit in a blender or food mill. Return to pot, add agar-agar and the 1 cup of juice, rind and cinnamon. Simmer uncovered for 20 minutes, stirring occasionally to prevent sticking. Use as a spread, pie filling or topping for muffins, cakes or breads. It can be stored in glass jars and kept in the refrigerator for about a week. A combination of dried fruit makes an interesting flavour. Arrowroot or kuzu can be used in place of agar (use about 2 tablespoons and reduce cooking time to 10 minutes).

Desserts

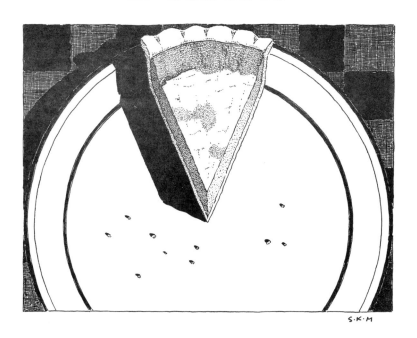

Desserts

Generally speaking, desserts are not an essential part of a meal and can actually upset a perfect balance achieved by the grains, vegetables and protein. They are best left for special occasions when they are really appreciated a lot more anyway. We have found that waiting an hour or so after a meal before eating fruit or something sweet works better digestion-wise.

Everyone has their favourite desserts. We have included a few simple versions with little or no sweetener and one or two which are perhaps a bit more complicated, but very special. The best recipe is the one you're using already. Just change the ingredients around. Substitute barley or rice malt for sugar, throw out the eggs and milk. Experiment! Here is a list of possible substitutes and conversions. Check the glossary at the back for terms.

Chocolate — Use carob powder or chips. Check carob chips for added sweeteners as some may contain sugar. Make a wet paste with a tiny bit of liquid when using carob powder. Slowly add more liquid using a blender.

sugar — barley or rice malt. 1 1/2 cups = 1 cup white sugar. 2/3 cups maple syrup or honey = 1 cup white sugar. Fruit juice is a good alternative sweetener. Adjust liquid accordingly or substitute the juice for other liquids called for. Most traditional recipes ask for excessive sugar. Usually 1/2 the amount will do.

cornstarch or flour thickeners — kudzu or arrowroot (see glossary). Dissolve 1 tbsp. per cup of liquid in cold water and simmer until mixture is clear and thickened.

gelatin — agar agar — available in flakes or bars and

sometimes in powder. Follow directions on package.

enriched white flour — unbleached white, whole wheat, rice, barley, ground oats, oat flakes, cornmeal, ground millet. Rice and barley flours make light pie crusts.

eggs — egg white or none at all.

milk — soya milk or water or tofu

buttermilk — soya milk soured with lemon

baking powder or baking soda — dry, bakers' yeast or sourdough starter (see.p. 98 for recipe)

butter, margarine — corn oil, tahini, nut butters — almond, cashew or peanut butter

home-made baking powder — most commercial brands contain sodium and aluminum. You can buy baking powder without these two ingredients in a pharmacy or health food store or make your own with 1 part potassium bicarbonate (available from a pharmacy), 2 parts cornstarch or arrowroot, and 2 parts cream of tartar. Sift three times and use according to recipe.

Apple Raisin Crisp

A very special Apple Betty that can be adapted to any fruit.

Topping

2 cups rolled oats
1/4 tsp. sea salt
1 cup chopped walnuts (or any nut-seed combination)
1/4 cup corn oil
1/2 cup barley malt

Mix oats, salt and nuts together. Add corn oil and mix well. Add barley malt to coat all ingredients. Set aside.

Filling

6 apples
a sprinkle of cinnamon
1 cup raisins, unsulphured

1 cup apple juice or cider
pinch sea salt
2 tbsp. kudzu diluted in 1/4 cup cold water *or cornstarch*

Wash, core and slice apples. Place in a baking dish and set aside. On top of stove, cook raisins in 1 cup apple juice with a pinch of sea salt until they are soft. Thicken with kudzu diluted in 1/4 cup of cold water. Pour raisin sauce over raw apples, sprinkle on topping and bake at 350^{0}F. for 40 minutes.

Strawberry-Apple Jello Kanten

This is an all-time favourite with the kids and has no added sweetener.

1 cup chopped apples and strawberries
2 cups water
2 cups apple juice, cider or strawberry/apple juice
pinch of sea salt
6 tbsp. agar agar flakes

Place juice, water and salt in a pot and bring to a boil. Add agar agar flakes and simmer gently until all flakes are dissolved. Remove from heat, add fruit and stir. Pour into a mold or flat pyrex cake dish. (Kanten seems to jell best in a flat dish). Cool in fridge until jelled.

Experiment with other fresh fruit in season and more or less juice according to your taste.

Dried Fruit Compote

This recipe can be adapted to fresh fruit. The amount of water used will then be just enough to keep the mixture from scorching, adding as you go along. Try other dried fruit as well.

1 cup raisins
1 cup dried apricots (unsulphured)
1 cup dried apples
water or apple cider
1/4 tsp. sea salt
1/2 cup kudzu (optional)

Place dried fruit in a pot and cover with water or juice. Bring to a boil and simmer on lowest heat for one hour until fruit is soft and dark-coloured. To thicken, dilute the kudzu in 5 tablespoons of cold water and stir slowly into the compote. Cook for one or two minutes longer. Serve warm or cool as a dessert or porridge companion. Yummy on toast.

Apple Sesame Custard (4-6 servings)

This is an all time favourite custard — super creamy and without eggs and milk. It was served recently at a wedding reception where it won hands down over its sugary rivals. We've tried it with pears with a wonderful cool taste. How about strawberries?

3-4 medium sized apples
1/2 cup raisins
2 cups apple cider or juice
2 cups water
2-3 tbsp. tahini
pinch of sea salt
5 tbsp. agar-agar flakes or 1 bar (see instructions on package)

Wash apples, peel if not organic, core them and slice. Place them in a fairly large pot with the juice, water, tahini, salt and agar. Stir, bring to a boil, lower heat and simmer 2-3 minutes. Pour mixture into a shallow bowl, such as a pyrex pie plate and chill until almost hardened. Place custard in a blender and blend until creamy. Return to serving dish and chill again before you serve it. Garnish with toasted, chopped almonds or walnuts.

Oatmeal Drop Cookies with a Twist
(About 1 dozen)

You can make these substituting rice malt for the maple syrup but they won't have that extra zip.

2 cups rolled oats
a couple pinches of sea salt
1/4 cup tahini
1/2 cup barley malt

1/4 cup maple syrup
1 1/4 tsp. pure vanilla
3 tbsp. water or fruit juice such as apple cider
1/3 cup tamari toasted sunflower seeds

Roast the sunflower seeds by heating on medium heat in a skillet until they turn brown and start to crackle. Spray or drop on tamari diluted with a miniscule amount of water — just enough to stop the spray nozzle from plugging up. Set aside the tamari seeds and combine the rest of the ingredients in a large bowl. Add the sunflower seeds and let this batter sit 1/2 hour or more. Place tin foil over an oven rack and oil well with sesame or corn oil. Drop cookies from a spoon onto the rack and shape them into medium size flattened rounds. Bake at 325⁰ for 25-30 minutes or until golden brown. Let cool slightly and then peel off the tin foil and transfer to a rack or plate to cool. Let sit for a half hour or so before devouring.

Muriel's Date Cookies

3 cups rolled oats
1 1/2 cups whole wheat pastry flour *or 1 1/4 cups regular w. w. flour*
pinch salt
3 tbsp. corn oil
3/4 tsp. vanilla
sprinkle of cinnamon
1/4 cup tahini
1/2 cup barley malt
3/4 cup chopped walnuts
3/4 chopped dates
2 cups water *only 1 cup water*

Mix dry ingredients. Add corn oil and mix well. Add vanilla and cinnamon. Dilute barley malt in 1/2 cup water. Add to other ingredients with another 1/2 cup water. Mix in dates and nuts and the remaining one cup water. Drop onto a cookie sheet and press down with a fork. Bake at 350⁰ for 20-25 minutes.

Almond-Raspberry Tart Cookies

1 cup ground almonds
1 cup ground rolled oats (blenderized)
1 cup whole wheat pastry flour
1/4 tsp. cinnamon
pinch sea salt
1/2 cup maple syrup or 1/4 cup rice malt and 1/4 cup maple syrup or 1/2 cup rice or barley malt
1/2 cup cold corn oil
6 oz raspberry jam, unsweetened or naturally sweetened

Combine dry and wet ingredients separately. Put the two together and mix as little as possible. Let rest 1/2 hour in refrigerator. Make small round balls and place on cookie sheet. Slightly flatten each ball by making a tiny indentation in the middle (a sterilized middle finger will do the trick). Add a drop or two of naturally sweetened raspberry jam. Bake at 350⁰ for 15 minutes. For variation use any other ground nuts or jam.

Krispie Kritters

A quick and easy solution to the cry for snacks.

1-1 1/2 cups rice krisps or puffed grain cereal (available packaged in most natural foods stores)
1 tbsp. tahini
1/4-1/2 cup rice syrup or barley malt
1/4-1/2 cup raisins and toasted, chopped almonds

Heat tahini and rice syrup until liquid. Pour over rice krisps, raisins and almonds and press into an oiled cake pan. Cool and cut into squares. Throw in those leftover rice cake crumbs. Delicious!

Tofu Ice Cream

Tofu ice cream is not generally recommended as a frequent dessert due to its highly "yin" or expansive nature. There is a product on the market made from amazake — a frozen rice cream which is of superior quality. However, as an occasional treat tofu ice cream is very cooling on a hot summer's day and delightfully clean.

2 lbs. soft tofu
1 and 1/3 cups soymilk
1 and 1/3 cups oil — safflower or sunflower
1-1 1/2 cups honey
1/4 cup fresh lemon juice
2 tbsp. vanilla
2 20 oz. cans of unsweetened pineapple, crushed with syrup

Blend in a blender in four equal parts the above ingredients, reserving 2 cups of drained pineapple to stir in before freezing. Add 1/4 tsp. salt to the total mixture before freezing. Freeze using a home ice cream maker.

For strawberry ice cream use 2 20 oz. packages of frozen unsweetened strawberries, 2 tbsp. vanilla and 1/3 cup soymilk less than above recipe.

Squash Pie

Makes one 10" pie. We used butternut but just about any other type of squash or yams will do.

Crust (or Pastry Pie Crust, p. 116)

1 1/2 cups of whole wheat pastry flour (or a combination of barley, rice and whole wheat)
pinch of sea salt
pinch of cinnamon
1/4 cup cold corn oil
approximately 1/4 cup cold water, very cold

Combine the flour, sea salt, cinnamon and sift together. Add the cold corn oil and rub between your hands until it looks like tiny pebbles. Add the cold water and mix quickly with a fork until the dough holds together and forms a ball. Roll out between waxed paper or press into a 10" pie pan. Make several holes with a fork in the bottom to allow steam to escape. Bake for 10 minutes at 350⁰.

Filling

2 1/2 lb. raw butternut squash

1/2 cup tahini
1 cup barley malt
1/2 tsp. cinnamon
pinch sea salt
1/2 tsp. ginger juice
1 1/2 tsp. agar powder or 1/2 oz. flakes
3 oz. apple juice or cider, unsweetened

Peel squash and cook for 30 minutes on low heat, or steam for 30 minutes until squashable. Grate a piece of ginger root and squeeze out 1/2 tsp. juice. Simmer 3 oz. of apple juice with the agar until the agar is dissolved. Let cool slightly. Blenderize all ingredients except the agar. Add the agar and blend again, briefly. Fill the prebaked pie shell and top with nuts. Bake at 350⁰ for 30-40 minutes until pie puffs up in centre. Cool for about two hours before serving.

Amasake Pudding

This is a wonderful custard-like dessert that is made from fermented rice called amasake. You can buy amasake ready-made in most health food stores but the homemade variety is not difficult to whip up and the taste is far superior. The big feature with amasake is its natural sweetness. The rice is fermented by adding a special starter called koji and a natural sugar is produced that is a real treat for those on sugar free diets.

Amasake syrup — blenderized amasake — can be used in any cake, cookie or bread recipe for added sweetness and leavening power. Adjust the liquid accordingly.

How to make amasake the easy way

4 cups sweet brown rice or 2 cups organic brown and 2 cups sweet
8 cups water
1/2 cup koji starter

Wash rice and soak overnight in the 8 cups of water. In the morning pressure cook for twenty minutes. Remove from heat and let sit for 45 minutes before removing the cover. Remove the rice and place in a large glass or porcelain bowl. When cool enough to handle, add the koji and mix in well. Cover with a wet cloth or bamboo mat and place in a warm oven (on pilot light) or near a radiator. Leave to ferment 4-8 hours stirring occasionally. (It's important to stir so as to continue the fermentation process). Place amasake in a large pot and bring to a boil. Simmer on lowest heat for 5-10 minutes, adding a bit of water if necessary to prevent scorching. Cool and store in glass jars in the refrigerator. It will keep up to two weeks.

Amasake Pudding (4-6 servings)

2 cups amasake concentrate, blenderized
1 1/2 cups apple cider or half water and half juice of your choice
4 tsp. kuzu
1/4 tsp. sea salt
2 tsp. agar flakes
1/2 tsp. pure vanilla
dried apricots, pears, apples — about 6 altogether

Soak the dried fruit about 10 minutes or until soft. Cut into tiny pieces. You may wish to use fresh fruit in season — 1/2 to 1 cup depending on size of fruit and your own taste. Combine the rest of the ingredients except for the vanilla in a medium-sized pot. Bring to a boil, stirring often. Reduce heat and simmer for 10 minutes, stirring occasionally. Add the fruit and vanilla and simmer on lowest heat for 3-5 minutes depending on which fruit you use. Remove from heat and place in a decorative bowl to cool. Chill in refrigerator or serve at room temperature. Decorate with roasted split almonds in flower shapes on the top of the pudding.

Christmas Pudding at the Quon's

This wonderful recipe was adapted by Pat Quon of Dartmouth, Nova Scotia. It is absolutely the best that we have ever tasted.

4 oz. whole wheat pastry flour
2 oz. bread crumbs
1 tsp. allspice
1 tsp. cinnamon
1 tsp. nutmeg
4 oz. corn oil (weigh it)
5 oz. barley malt
1 grated apple
1 small grated carrot
4 oz. currants
8 oz. raisins
4 oz. sultanas
6 oz. dried apricots (chopped)
4 oz. chopped walnuts or almonds
grated rind of 1/2 lemon
juice of 1/2 lemon
1/4 pint ale, beer or stout

Mix all ingredients together, stir well and leave overnight. Place mixture in 1 large or 2 smaller oiled stainless steel bowls. Cover with 2 or 3 layers of wax paper, then 1 layer of foil, making sure to get the foil snug. Steam or boil for 6-8 hours. Cool. Remove wet covering. When cold, put on dry covers. Store in fridge until needed — then steam for 2 hours. Serve with either a hot vanilla sauce or a hard sauce.

Vanilla Sauce

1/4 cup whole oat flour
2 tbsp. short grain brown rice flour
2 1/2 tbsp. agar agar flakes
pinch sea salt
2 1/4 cups water
2 tbsp. rice syrup
3 tbsp. maple syrup

2 1/2 tsp. pure vanilla

Blenderize oat flakes until they become a fine powder. Sift out the excess bran to make 1/4 cup flour. In a medium saucepan combine the flours, agar-agar and salt. Add the water and mix together well. Bring to a boil; stir often. Reduce flame and simmer for 10 minutes, again stirring often. Remove from heat when agar is dissolved. Add remaining ingredients and blend in blender until smooth. Add enough extra water to make a thick pourable sauce. Serve hot or cold over Xmas pudding or as a separate dessert pudding, keep water at 2 1/4 cups for a thicker consistency.

Lemon Meringue Pie (6-8 servings)
Filling

4 tbsp. arrowroot flour starch or kuzu
4 tbsp. unbleached white flour or sweet rice flour
    or
4 tbsp. kuzu and   *or cornstarch or arrow root Powder*
4 tbsp. agar flakes
1/2 cup cold apple juice
1/8 tsp. sea salt
1 1/4 cups boiling apple juice
1/2 cup amasake syrup or rice malt or 3 tsp. maple syrup
3 egg yolks, well beaten   *4*
rind and juice of 2 lemons
1 tbsp. corn oil

Meringue

3 egg whites
pinch salt
1 tbsp. amasake syrup or rice malt

Crust

Whole wheat piecrust, baked for 10 minutes (p. 116)

Mix together arrowroot and flour in 1/2 cup cold apple juice in a saucepan. Add salt, boiling apple juice and rice malt, beating well with a whisk. Simmer ever so gently over a double boiler or flame tamer for 10-15 minutes. (If using agar, add flakes to

115

hot mixture and simmer). Beat in egg yolks quickly, then add lemon rind and juice. Remove from heat and let cool. Beat together egg whites, salt and rice malt until stiff. Pour filling into baked crust and let it set. Top with meringue and bake for 10-15 minutes or until meringue is lightly browned. If pie does not set immediately, place in fridge and hold off on the meringue until the lemon part sets. Let the pie crust cool about 20 minutes before adding the filling.

Pastry Pie Crust

1 1/2 cups whole wheat pastry flour
1/4 tsp. sea salt
1/4 cup corn oil
6-7 tbsp. water

Combine the flour and salt. With a fork, slowly mix in the oil and the water. The dough should be a bit crumbly. Gather into a firm ball. Leave in the bowl and cover with a damp towel. Refrigerate twenty minutes. Roll out to a 10 or 11 inch diameter. Place in a pyrex pie plate. Prick bottom and sides with a fork. Bake on lower shelf for about 30 minutes or until golden brown.

Glossary

Agar-agar
Available in bars, flakes and powder. A gelatin-like substance derived from a sea vegetable and used in making jelled dishes and puddings. Comparable to gelatin which is an animal food product.

Arrowroot —
A starch flour used to thicken sauces, stews, desserts, etc. Like cornstarch, it must be diluted in cold water before adding to hot liquids.

Azuki or aduki beans —
Small, red Japanese beans, which are also cultivated in North America. They are very "yang," compact and powerful.

Cattle Beans —
Beige and black speckled bean, good in soups and casseroles.

Chickpeas or garbanzos —
A light brown bean shaped like an irregular rough-edged pea

Groats —
A name given to certain whole grains such as oats, rye or buckwheat.

Kuzu or kudzu —
Made from the wild arrowroot plant, a white chalky substance that thickens while it soothes. Very good for intestinal flora. Dissolve in cold liquid first and use as cornstarch.

Lentils —
A flat, greenish brown bean grown in North America. Also found as a smaller orange variety.

Marinate —
To soak certain foods such as fish, vegetables or tofu in a liquid.

Matchsticks —
A style of cutting vegetables by slicing first on the diagonal and then chopping into thin strips resembling the end of a wooden match.

Matzoh meal —
Crushed matzoh, a Jewish unleavened bread

Mirin —
A sweet, cooking wine made from sweet rice.

Mochi cubes —
A dumpling-like substance made from pounded sweet rice.

Mu tea —
A flavourful tea made from a variety of herbs.

Oxydizing —
Exposure to air or the oxygen present in air. Oxydizing can produce nutritional loss in foods.

Pinto beans —
Brown, speckled beans from southern United States.

Pressure Cooker —
Stainless steel are the best. Cuts cooking time for beans and whole grains and allows food to retain vitamins and minerals. Simple and easy to use following manufacturer's instructions.

Proofing —
Allowing bread to ferment or rise for several hours after kneading.

Sesame oil —
Oil extracted from sesame seeds, (cold pressed, unrefined oil is recommended for the most nutritive value).

Shitake Mushrooms —
A Japanese mushroom usually found packaged and dried. A unique sweet taste adds incredible flavour to soups, stews and sea vegetable dishes.

Soba —
Noodles made from 100% buckwheat flour or a combination of buckwheat and other flours. Very warming, a good winter food.

Suribachi—
A Japanese pottery bowl with tiny ridges on the inside. Used much like a mortar and pestle on a larger scale for blending sauces and puréeing food.

Tahini —
A smooth paste made from ground white sesame seeds. Fairly oily; delicious in sauces and spreads.

Tamari sauce —
A natural, unprocessed soya sauce made from fermented soy beans, wheat and sea salt. Wheat free tamari is also available.

Umeboshi plum —
A salty, pickled plum with wonderful soothing effects on the digestive system.

Ume or umeboshi vinegar —
A vinegar made using the umeboshi plum.

Yang —
One of the two basic energies at work in the universe. Manifests as heat, light, denseness, inward and in foods as compact grains such as rice, buckwheat and millet, beans, root vegetables and salt. A contracting, tightening force.

Yin —
The complement to the yang force in the universe. Represented by expansion, lightness, airy, cold, dark, upward and outward energy. Present in food as leafy vegetables, lighter grains — corn, oats, barley, bulgur, oils, nuts, fruit and liquid.

Bibliography

+*** *Complete Guide to Macrobiotic Cooking* by Aveline Kushi.

+** *Diet for a Small Planet* by Frances Moore Lappe

+*** *East West Journal* by Kushi Foundation Ltd., a monthly magazine

+*** *Introducing Macrobiotic Cooking* by Wendy Esko

+** *Laurel's Kitchen* by Robertson, Flinders and Godfrey

+ *Let's Eat Right to Keep Fit* by Adelle Davis

+*** *Macrobiotic Cooking for Everyone* by Edward and Wendy Esko

+*** *MacroMuse*, The Macrobiotic Forum Magazine of Bethesda, Maryland

+ *Nutrition Almanac* by John Kirschman, Director

** *Recipes for a Small Planet* by Frances Moore Lappe

+** *Sea Green Primer* by Juel Andersen

+ *Sunset Menus and Recipes for Vegetarian Cooking*, Sunset Books

+*** *Ten Talents* by Frank and Rosalie Hurd

+** *The Book of Tofu* by Shurtleff and Aoyagi

+** *The Book of Whole Foods* by Karen MacNeil

*** *The Book of Whole Meals* by Annemarie Colbin

* *The Enchanted Broccoli Forest* by Mollie Katzen

** *The Moosewood Cookbook* by Mollie Katzen

** *The New York Times Cookbook* by Jean Hewitt

* *The Vegetarian Epicure*, Books 1 and 2 by Anna Thomas

** *Tofu Cookery* by Louise Hagler

+** *Vegetarian Times.* P.O. Box 570, Oak Park, Illinois 60303

*** *Whole World Cookbook* by the Editors of the East West Journal